F1 2000

Michael Schumacher and Ferrari won the last world championship of the millennium. It was a championship dominated by technology, stratospheric budgets, electronics, wind-tunnels and 'robot-drivers' who the fans can only 'see' on television or 'hear' through 'PR-speak' press releases. But in this super-sophisticated world, victory above all went to Maranello, a sleepy town of 15,000 inhabitants, and a company where its employees still today speak in dialect. Those are the same employees who demanded the dismissal of their famous chief designer a few years ago because he had banned them from drinking wine during the lunch break! It is with this spirit that the curtain is drawn on the final championship of the millennium, a spirit that will surely be appreciated by Ferrari's great rivals after their initial disappointment has faded away. Thanks to McLaren and Hakkinen for keeping alive this exciting world championship right to the very end!

Fotografia
Photography
Fotografie

BRYN WILLIAMS -
GRAEME BROWN, PAOLO D'ALESSIO, FERRARI UFF. STAMPA, CHARLES B-KNIGHT, FRITS VAN ELDIK

Disegni tecnici
Cutaways
Illustrationen
Illustraties

PAOLO D'ALESSIO

Realizzazione grafica
Graphic realization
Grafische vormgeving

DIEGO GALBIATI

Coordinamento tecnico
Technical coordinator

ERMENEGILDO CHIOZZOTTO

Traduzioni
Translations
Übersetzung
Vertaling

JULIAN THOMAS
OLAV MOL , RICK WINKELMAN
NICOLAUS C. KORETZKY

Fotolito
Colour separations
Reproduktion
Fotolitho's

FOTOLITO FB - TORINO (ITALY)

Stampa
Printing
Druck
Druk

INDUSTRIE ARTI GRAFICHE GARZANTI VERGA
CERNUSCO S. N. (MILANO - ITALY)

Realizzazione
Editorial production
Herstellungskoordination
Redactie en samenstelling

SEP EDITRICE - CERNUSCO S. N. (MILANO - ITALY)

Printed in Italy - October 2000

Si ringrazia
AUTOSPRINT
settimanale di automobilismo sportivo leader in Italia,
fonte inesauribile di informazioni e dati statistici ripresi per questo libro.

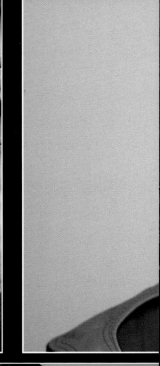

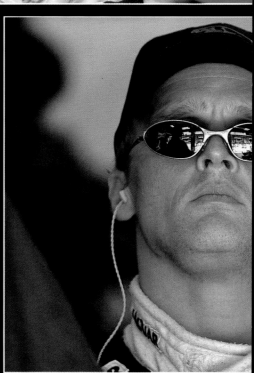

14

16

Magny-Cours • M. Schumacher - D. Coulthard

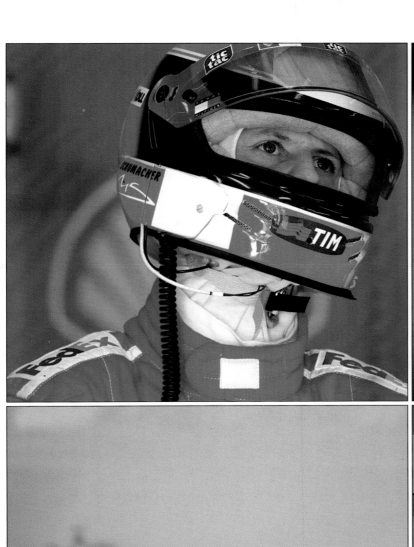

Alexander Wurz (Benetton)

Jarno Trulli (Jordan) 33

36   **Ricardo Zonta (BAR)**

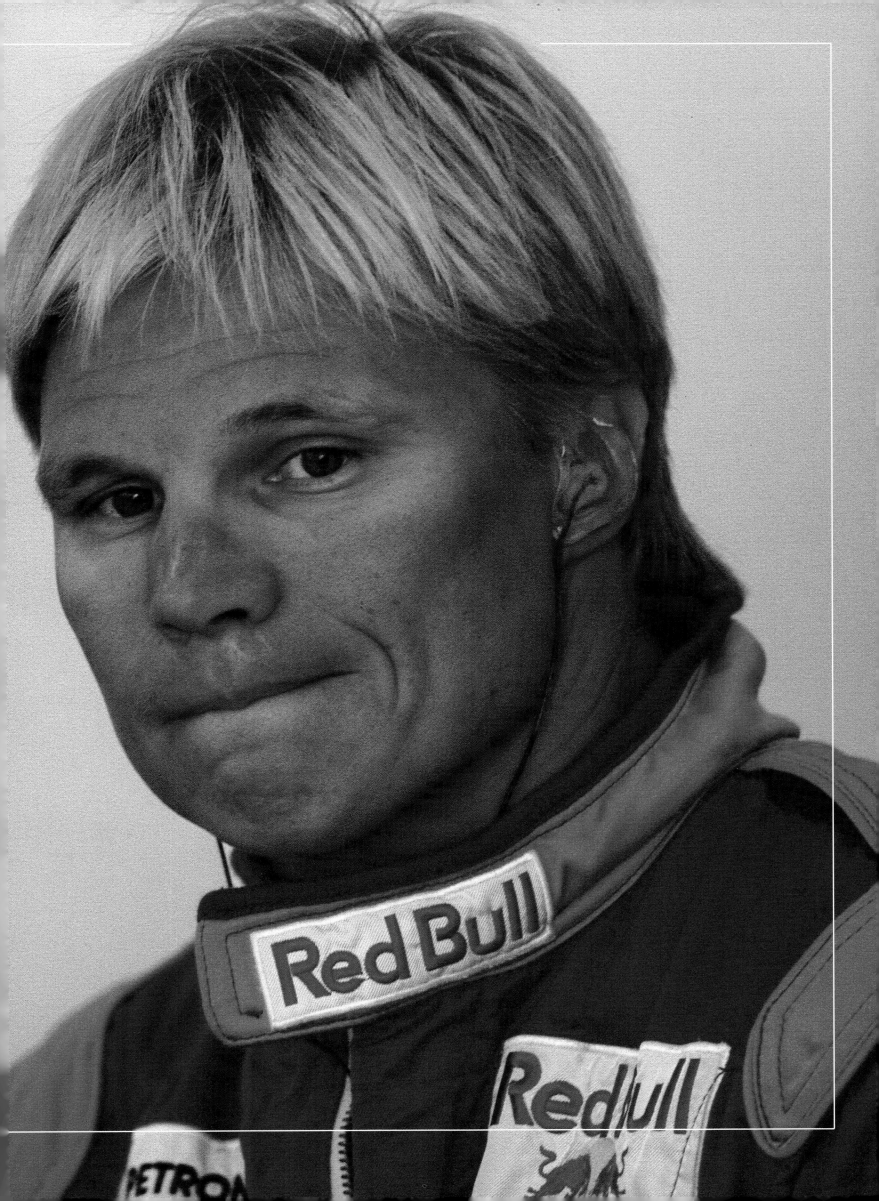

48   **Jenson Button (Williams)**

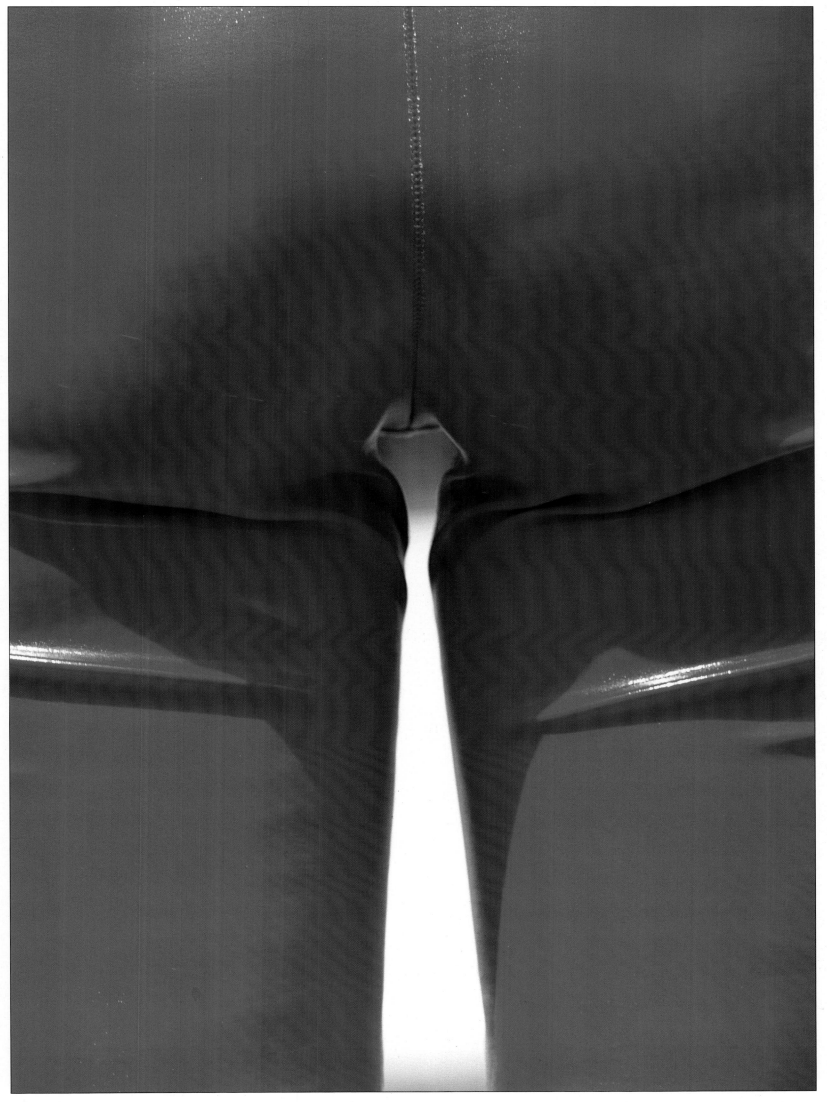

Craig Pollock (BAR)

Sarah Ferguson

L. di Montezemolo - Claudio Berro (Ferrari)

Flavio Briatore (Benetton) - Bernie Ecclestone

Eddie Jordan

Paul Stewart

Naomi Campbell

Gerard Berger (BMW) - Patrick Head (Williams)

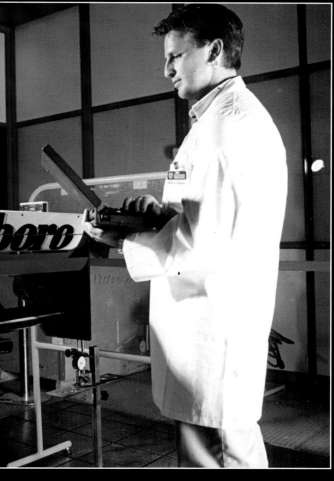

1/16
The Ferrari-McLaren battle resumed in 2000, with the only change being Rubens Barrichello who gave a big hand to the Prancing Horse's *efforts* to win the Constructors' championship.

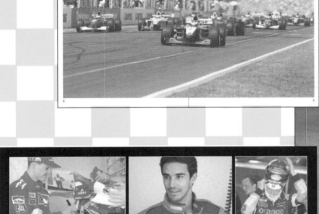

17
Welcome back F1!
The 2000 championship
saw a continuation
of the duel between Ferrari
and McLaren. In the photo:
the start of the French GP
with Schumacher on pole
ahead of Coulthard.

18/19
Mika Hakkinen
at Monte Carlo.
It was a weekend to forget
for the Finn who qualified
5th and finished 6th.

20/21
David Coulthard, 29,
has been Mika Hakkinen's
team-mate in McLaren
since 1996.
The Scot has been
reconfirmed for next
year as well.

22/23
Rubens Barrichello
retired from the Belgian GP
ten laps from the end after
running out of fuel at
the pit lane entry.

24/25
The backdrop
to every Grand Prix.
Final preparations on
the track and tension in
the Ferrari pit garage.

26/27
Alexander Wurz
made his F1 debut
with Benetton in the 1997
Canadian GP.

28/29
The Benetton team
was sold off to the
Renault Group this year.
It will continue to be called
Benetton until the end
of next season, when it will
become Team Renault.

32
It was a difficult year
for Jordan despite
the team having
two of the fastest
drivers around: veteran
Heinz-Harald Frentzen
and rising star Jarno Trulli.

30/31
Monaco - Jos Verstappen
(Arrows A21).

33
Jarno Trulli
(Jordan EJ 10).

34/35
Jaguar-Ford made an important return to top-level motorsport in 2000, but it will take time before concrete results can be achieved.

36/37
Jacques Villeneuve decided to stay with BAR for another year in 2001, despite his fluctuating fortunes in this year's championship.

38/39
Not much can be said about Prost Grand Prix. Luckily, in veteran Jean Alesi his team has a great driver and a wonderful personality.

40/41
Finn Mika Salo joins Toyota as test-driver next year as the Japanese manufacturer gears up for F1 entry in 2002.

42/43
Minardi has been in F1 for 15 years and has taken part in more than 250 GPs. This is a major achievement for the small Italian team, which has launched a number of talented drivers in the past.

44/45
It was a fantastic return to F1 for Jos Verstappen (Arrows), who produced some superb performances throughout the year.

46/47
Ralf Schumacher confirmed that he was one of F1's top drivers and the German took his surprising BMW-Williams to numerous podium finishes throughout the season.

48
The final page of this photo gallery belongs to Jenson Button who made a superb debut in Formula One this year.

50/51
Today's Formula One teams are embarking on a race to see which one has the most expensive and spectacular motorhome.
Some drivers, such as Schumacher and Barrichello, even bring along a mobile gym to keep fit.

52/53
The years go by, but the paddock world remains the same. Briatore's companion, top model Naomi Campbell, is the latest arrival.

54/55
When the engine noise dies down and the VIPs retire to the motorhomes, the paddock is once again the home of the mechanics and the engineers.

56/57
Jaguar's amazing motorhome.

58/59
More than 200 fire marshals are on duty at every circuit. At Monza, as well as Imola, the service is carried out by the famous 'CEA Lions', who pulled Gerhard Berger out of the flames at Imola in 1989.

60/61
Behind the scenes in F1. A look at the activity in the Ferrari factory and behind the pit garage.

62/63
In the circuits, the pit garages are increasingly beginning to look like luxurious showrooms.
In the photo: the Minardi pit garage.

64
Ricardo Zonta (Arrows A21).

FORMULA 1 CALENDAR 2000

12 March

The BMW engine makes its debut in Australia with Williams and Ralf Schumacher finishes 3rd - first race and first podium.

16 March

The Benetton family bows out of F1 after 14 years following its buyout by Renault. Flavio Briatore returns to head the team.

7 April

Minardi celebrates its 15th birthday. The Italian team made its debut on April 7, 1985 in the Brazilian GP with Pierluigi Martini.

9 April

Eddie Irvine and HH Frentzen both celebrated their 100th GP at Imola. The record holder is Italian Riccardo Patrese with 256 GPs.

Jordan 1991

23 April

Jordan Grand Prix celebrated its 150th GP at Silverstone. It made its debut in the 1991 United States GP with Andrea de Cesaris and Bertrand Gachot.

7 May

36 year-old Johnny Herbert notches up his 150th GP. He made his debut with a Benetton in the 1989 Brazilian GP.

21 May

Jarno Trulli (Jordan) celebrated his 50th GP at the Nürburgring.

21 May

Ferrari is 50 years old today. It made its debut in 1950 with Alberto Ascari at Monte Carlo.

4 June

Jaguar scores its first points in F1 with fourth place for Irvine in the Monaco GP.

4 June

A fantastic front-row grid position for Italian Jarno Trulli with a Jordan at Monte Carlo.

Monaco 1966

18 June

In Canada McLaren celebrated its 500th race in F1. It made its debut at Monte Carlo in 1966.

16 July

Brazil's Luciano Burti, 25, made his debut in Austria as one-race substitute for Irvine.

23 July

Rubens Barrichello scored his first win in a Ferrari at the German GP.

17 August

Benetton confirmed that Jenson Button and Giancarlo Fisichella would drive for the team in 2001.

27 August

Minardi celebrated its 250th GP at Spa.

29 August

Daniele Amaduzzi, one of the most well-known photographers in Formula 1, died at the age of 52. He was not just a great photographer, but also one of the last remaining characters from a time when F1 was a lot more romantic and closer to the fans that it is today.

10 September

Honda notched up 200 races for its engines in F1 at the Monza circuit.

10 September

Jaguar announced that Eddie Irvine and Luciano Burti would be the team's drivers in 2001.

10 September

A fire marshal was killed after being hit by a wheel from Frentzen's Jordan during lap 1 of the Italian GP.

22 September

Alain Prost announced that he has signed an engine supply deal with Ferrari for his team in the 2001 championship.

5 October

Tomas Scheckter, the 20-year-old son of 1979 World Champion Jody Scheckter, has signed as Jaguar Racing test driver for the 2001 season. He replaces Luciano Burti.

1959 2000

Back in the USA

Bruce McLaren, driving a Cooper T45-Climax, was the winner of the first United States GP,
which was held on the disused concrete runways of Hendricks Field near Sebring, Florida in 1959.
It was a lucky victory for the 22 year-old New Zealander, who became the youngest
ever GP winner after Jack Brabham ran out of fuel in the closing laps.
The race was poorly attended and moved to Riverside, California the following year.
Stirling Moss won the final race for 2.5-litre cars in a Lotus 18-Climax and it was also
the final race for Maserati with its 250F.
In 1961 it was the turn of Watkins Glen to host the grand prix, which was won by Innes Ireland
in a Lotus 21-Climax. That was a tragic year for Formula 1 however because of the death
of Wolfgang Von Trips and fourteen spectators at Monza following a collision with Jim Clark's
Lotus at the Parabolica. Clark won the United States GP in 1962 at Watkins Glen,
where the race would be held every year until 1980.
Graham Hill (BRM) dominated the United States GP for the next three years, taking a hat-trick
of victories in 1963, 1964 and 1965. In that year (1965) his great rival Jim Clark won
the Indianapolis 500 Miles, the first European to taste victory at the Brickyard,
and he was imitated the following year by Graham Hill, with Clark finishing second.
But Clark won the next two United States GPs in 1966 and 1967 with a Lotus.
The 1968 race will be remembered for the first pole position in F1 by an American driver,
Mario Andretti, who was making his debut in that race.
1968 was a tumultuous year for F1. It started off with the introduction of commercial sponsorship
to Grand Prix racing, when Team Lotus repainted its cars red and white in deference to Gold Leaf
cigarettes. It continued with the introduction of aerodynamic wings but the sport was sent into
a state of shock with the deaths of Jim Clark at Hockenheim, Ludovico Scarfiotti in a hill climb,
Mike Spence at Indianapolis and Jo Schlesser on his debut at the French GP in a Honda.
In 1969 Jochen Rindt won his first F1 race at Watkins Glen after setting pole position.
The Austrian took the chequered flag after a superb battle with eventual champion Jackie Stewart.
Rindt became the first and only posthumous champion in F1 history the following year when
he died after crashing his Lotus 72 at the Parabolica in Italian GP practice.
In 1976 the United States GP doubled up with two races per season and this tradition was
to continue until the 1984 season.

The permanent venue for the United States GP (West) until 1983 became Long Beach,
California, while the second GP was held at Watkins Glen (from 1976 to 1980),
Las Vegas (1981 and 1982), Detroit (1983 and 1984) and finally Dallas (1984).
Three drivers scored double wins the same year in the United States:
Ferrari's Carlos Reutemann in 1978 and Gilles Villeneuve in 1979,
and Alan Jones in 1981 for Williams.

In the 1976 United States GP at Watkins Glen, Jody Scheckter finished runner-up with the revolutionary Tyrrell P34 six-wheel car, while in 1980 at the Long Beach circuit, Swiss driver Clay Regazzoni was seriously injured and paralysed from the waist down when his Ensign crashed into a retired car. 1985 saw a return to just one United States GP, in Detroit, a race won by Finland's Keke Rosberg. The world's automobile capital remained the venue for the United States GP until 1988 and saw three successive wins for Ayrton Senna with a Lotus in 1986 and 1987, and with a McLaren in 1988, the year in which the British team won 15 out of 16 GPs. The only exception was the Italian GP where Ferrari scored a 1-2 with Gerhard Berger and Michele Alboreto.

In 1989 the United States GP was moved to Phoenix, Arizona where it remained until 1991, the last time it was run until Indianapolis 2000.

The circuit was the same and so was the name of the winning car – McLaren – with victories for Alain Prost in 1989 and Ayrton Senna in 1990 and 1991.

1959

Bruce McLaren
(Cooper-Climax)

STARTING-GRID FOR THE FIRST-EVER UNITED STATES GP

Stirling Moss	**Jack Brabham**	**Harry Schell**
Cooper-Climax T51	Cooper-Climax T51	Cooper-Climax T51
3'00"0	3'03"0	3'05"2

Tony Brooks	**Maurice Trintignant**
Ferrari 246	Cooper-Climax T51
3'05"9	3'06"0

Wolfgang Von Trips	**Cliff Allison**	**Phil Hill**
Ferrari 246	Ferrari 246	Ferrari 246
3'06"2	3'06"8	3'07"2

Innes Ireland	**Bruce McLaren**
Lotus-Climax 16	Cooper-Climax T51
3'08"2	3'08"6

Roy Salvadori	**Alan Stacey**	**Bob Said**
Cooper-Maserati	Lotus-Climax 16	Connaught
3'12"0	3'13"8	3'27"3

Alejandro De Tomaso	**George Costantine**
Cooper-Osca F.2	Cooper-Climax T51
3'28"0	3'30"6

Harry Blanchard	**Fritz D'Orey**	**Rodger Ward**
Porsche RSK	Tec Mec-Maserati	Kurtis-Offenhauser
3'32"7	3'33"4	3'43"8

RESULT

1. McLaren (Cooper-Climax) av. speed kph 159,06 km/h;
2. Trintignant (Cooper-Climax); 3. Brooks (Ferrari);
4. Brabham (Cooper-Climax); 5. Ireland (Lotus-Climax);
6. Von Trips (Ferrari); 7. Blanchard (Porsche RSK).

12.12.1959
GP USA - Sebring
Pole Position: S. Moss
Podium
1. Bruce McLaren - Cooper Climax
2. Maurice Trintignant - Cooper Climax
3. Tony Brooks - Ferrari

20.11.1960
GP USA - Riverside
Pole Position: S. Moss
Podium
1. Stirling Moss - Lotus Climax
2. Innes Ireland - Lotus Climax
3. Bruce McLaren - Cooper Climax

08.11.1961
GP USA - Watkins Glen
Pole Position: J. Brabham
Podium
1. Innes Ireland - Lotus Climax
2. Dan Gurney - Porsche
3. Tony Brooks - BRM

07.10.1962
GP USA - Watkins Glen
Pole Position: J. Clark
Podium
1. Jim Clark - Lotus Climax
2. Graham Hill - BRM
3. Bruce McLaren - Cooper Climax

06.10.1963
GP USA - Watkins Glen
Pole Position: G. Hill
Podium
1. Graham Hill - BRM
2. Richie Ginther - BRM
3. Jim Clark - Lotus Climax

04.10.1964
GP USA - Watkins Glen
Pole Position: J. Clark
Podium
1. Graham Hill - BRM
2. John Surtees - Ferrari
3. Joseph Siffert - Brabham BRM

03.10.1965
GP USA - Watkins Glen
Pole Position: G. Hill
Podium
1. Graham Hill - BRM
2. Dan Gurney - Brabham Climax
3. Jack Brabham - Brabham Climax

02.10.1966
GP USA - Watkins Glen
Pole Position: J. Brabham
Podium
1. Jim Clark - Lotus-BRM
2. Jochen Rindt - Cooper Maserati
3. John Surtees - Cooper Maserati

01.10.1967
GP USA - Watkins Glen
Pole Position: G. Hill
Podium
1. Jim Clark - Lotus Ford
2. Graham Hill - Lotus Ford
3. Denis Hulme - Brabham Repco

06.10.1968
GP USA - Watkins Glen
Pole Position: M. Andretti
Podium
1. Jackie Stewart - Matra Ford
2. Graham Hill - Lotus Ford
3. John Surtees - Honda

05.10.1969
GP USA - Watkins Glen
Pole Position: J. Rindt
Podium
1. Jochen Rindt - Lotus Ford
2. Piers Courage - Brabham Ford
3. John Surtees - BRM

04.10.1970
GP USA - Watkins Glen
Pole Position: J. Ickx
Podium
1. Emerson Fittipaldi - Lotus Ford
2. Pedro Rodriguez - BRM
3. Reine Wisel - Lotus Ford

03.10.1971
GP USA - Watkins Glen
Pole Position: J. Stewart
Podium
1. François Cevert - Tyrrell Ford
2. Joseph Siffert - BRM
3. Ronnie Peterson - March Ford

08.10.1972
GP USA - Watkins Glen
Pole Position: J. Stewart
Podium
1. Jackie Stewart - Tyrrell Ford
2. FFrançois Cevert - Tyrrell Ford
3. Denis Hulme - McLaren Ford

07.10.1973
GP USA - Watkins Glen
Pole Position: R. Peterson
Podium
1. Ronnie Peterson - Lotus Ford
2. James Hunt - March Ford
3. Carlos Reutemann - Brabham Ford

06.10.1974
GP USA - Watkins Glen
Pole Position: C. Reutemann
Podium
1. Carlos Reutemann - Brabham Ford
2. Carlos Pace - Brabham Ford
3. James Hunt - Hesketh Ford

05.10.1975
GP USA - Watkins Glen
Pole Position: N. Lauda
Podium
1. Niki Lauda - Ferrari
2. Emerson Fittipaldi - McLaren Ford
3. Jochen Mass - McLaren Ford

28.03.1976
GP USA West - Long Beach
Pole Position: C. Regazzoni
Podium
1. Clay Regazzoni - Ferrari
2. Niki Lauda - Ferrari
3. Patrick Depailler - Tyrrell Ford

10.10.1976
GP USA - Watkins Glen
Pole Position: J. Hunt
Podium
1. James Hunt - McLaren Ford
2. Jody Schecker - Tyrrell Ford
3. Niki Lauda - Ferrari

03.04.1977
GP USA West- Long Beach
Pole Position: N. Lauda
Podium
1. Mario Andretti - Lotus Ford
2. Niki Lauda - Ferrari
3. Jody Schecker - Wolf Ford

02.10.1977
GP USA - Watkins Glen
Pole Position: J. Hunt
Podium
1. James Hunt - McLaren Ford
2. Mario Andretti - Lotus Ford
3. Jody Schecker - Wolf Ford

02.04.1978
GP USA West- Long Beach
Pole Position: C. Reutemann
Podium
1. Carlos Reutemann - Ferrari
2. Mario Andretti - Lotus Ford
3. Patrick Depailler - Tyrrell Ford

01.10.1978
GP USA - Watkins Glen
Pole Position: M. Andretti
Podium
1. Carlos Reutemann - Ferrari
2. Alan Jones - Williams Ford
3. Jody Scheckter - Wolf Ford

08.04.1979
GP USA West - Long Beach
Pole Position: G. Villeneuve
Podium
1. Gilles Villeneuve - Ferrari
2. Jody Scheckter - Ferrari
3. Alan Jones - Williams Ford

▲ **1979 G. Villeneuve (Ferrari) - J. Laffite (Ligier Matra)**

76

▼ **1980 Long Beach - J. Scheckter (Ferrari)**

07.10.1979
GP USA - Watkins Glen
Pole Position: A. Jones
Podium
1. Gilles Villeneuve - Ferrari
2. René Arnoux - Renault
3. Didier Pironi - Tyrrell Ford

30.03.1980
GP USA West- Long Beach
Pole Position: N. Piquet
Podium
1. Nelson Piquet - Brabham Ford
2. Riccardo Patrese - Arrows Ford
3. Emerson Fittipaldi - Fittipaldi Ford

05.10.1980
GP USA - Watkins Glen
Pole Position: B. Giacomelli
Podium
1. Alan Jones - Williams Ford
2. Carlos Reutemann - Williams Ford
3. Didier Pironi - Ligier Ford

15.03.1981
GP USA West- Long Beach
Pole Position: R. Patrese
Podium
1. Alan Jones - Williams Ford
2. Carlos Reutemann - Williams Ford
3. Nelson Piquet - Brabham Ford

17.10.1981
GP USA - Las Vegas
Pole Position: C. Reutemann
Podium
1. Alan Jones - Williams Ford
2. Alain Prost - Renault
3. Bruno Giacomelli - Alfa Romeo

04.04.1982
GP USA West- Long Beach
Pole Position: A. de Cesaris
Podium
1. Niki Lauda - McLaren Ford
2. Keke Rosberg - Williams Ford
3. Riccardo Patrese - Brabham Ford

▲ **1980 Long Beach - Ken Tyrrell**   ▲ **1982 Nigel Mansell**

▲ **1982 Long Beach - Didier Pironi (Ferrari)**

78

25.09.1982
GP USA - Las Vegas
Pole Position: A. Prost
Podium
1. Michele Alboreto - Tyrrell Ford
2. John Watson - McLaren Ford
3. Eddie Cheever - Talbot Ligier Matra

27.03.1983
GP USA West- Long Beach
Pole Position: P. Tambay
Podium
1. John Watson - McLaren Ford
2. Niki Lauda - McLaren Ford
3. René Arnoux - Ferrari

05.06.1983
GP USA- Detroit
Pole Position: R. Arnoux
Podium
1. Michele Alboreto - Tyrrell Ford
2. Keke Rosberg - Williams Ford
3. John Watson - McLaren Ford

24.06.1984
GP USA - Detroit
Pole Position: N. Piquet
Podium
1. Nelson Piquet - Brabham BMW
2. Elio de Angelis - Lotus Renault
3. Teo Fabi - Brabham Ford

08.07.1984
GP USA - Dallas
Pole Position: N. Mansell
Podium
1. Keke Rosberg - Williams Honda
2. René Arnoux - Ferrari
3. Elio de Angelis - Lotus Renault

23.06.1985
GP USA - Detroit
Pole Position: A. Senna
Podium
1. Keke Rosberg - Williams Honda
2. Stefan Johansson - Ferrari
3. Michele Alboreto - Ferrari

22.06.1986
GP USA - Detroit
Pole Position: A. Senna
Podium
1. Ayrton Senna - Lotus Renault
2. Jacques Laffite - Ligier Renault
3. Alain Prost - McLaren Porsche

▲ 1990 Phoenix - Ayrton Senna (McLaren Honda)

▲ 1991 Phoenix - Mika Hakkinen (Lotus Judd)

21.06.1987
GP USA - Detroit
Pole Position: N. Mansell
Podium
1. Ayrton Senna - Lotus Honda
2. Nelson Piquet - Williams Honda
3. Alain Prost - McLaren Porsche

19.06.1988
GP USA - Detroit
Pole Position: A. Senna
Podium
1. Ayrton Senna - McLaren Honda
2. Alain Prost - McLaren Honda
3. Thierry Boutsen - Benetton Ford

04.06.1989
GP USA - Phoenix
Pole Position: A. Senna
Podium
1. Alain Prost - McLaren Honda
2. Riccardo Patrese - Williams Renault
3. Eddie Cheever - Arrows Ford

11.03.1990
GP USA - Phoenix
Pole Position: G. Berger
Podium
1. Ayrton Senna - McLaren Honda
2. Jean Alesi - Tyrrell Ford
3. Thierry Boutsen - Williams Renault

10.03.1991
GP USA - Phoenix
Pole Position: A. Senna
Podium
1. Ayrton Senna - McLaren Honda
2. Alain Prost - Ferrari
3. Nelson Piquet - Benetton Ford

24.09.2000
GP USA - Indianapolis
Pole Position: M. Schumacher
Podium
1. Michael Schumacher - Ferrari
2. Rubens Barrichello - Ferrari
3. Heinz Harald Frentzen - Jordan

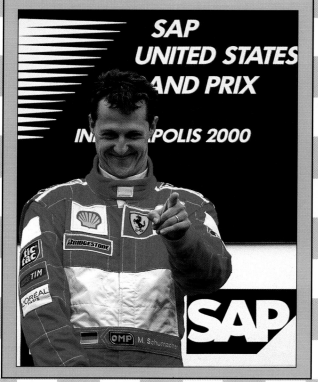

SAP UNITED STATES GRAND PRIX
INDIANAPOLIS 2000

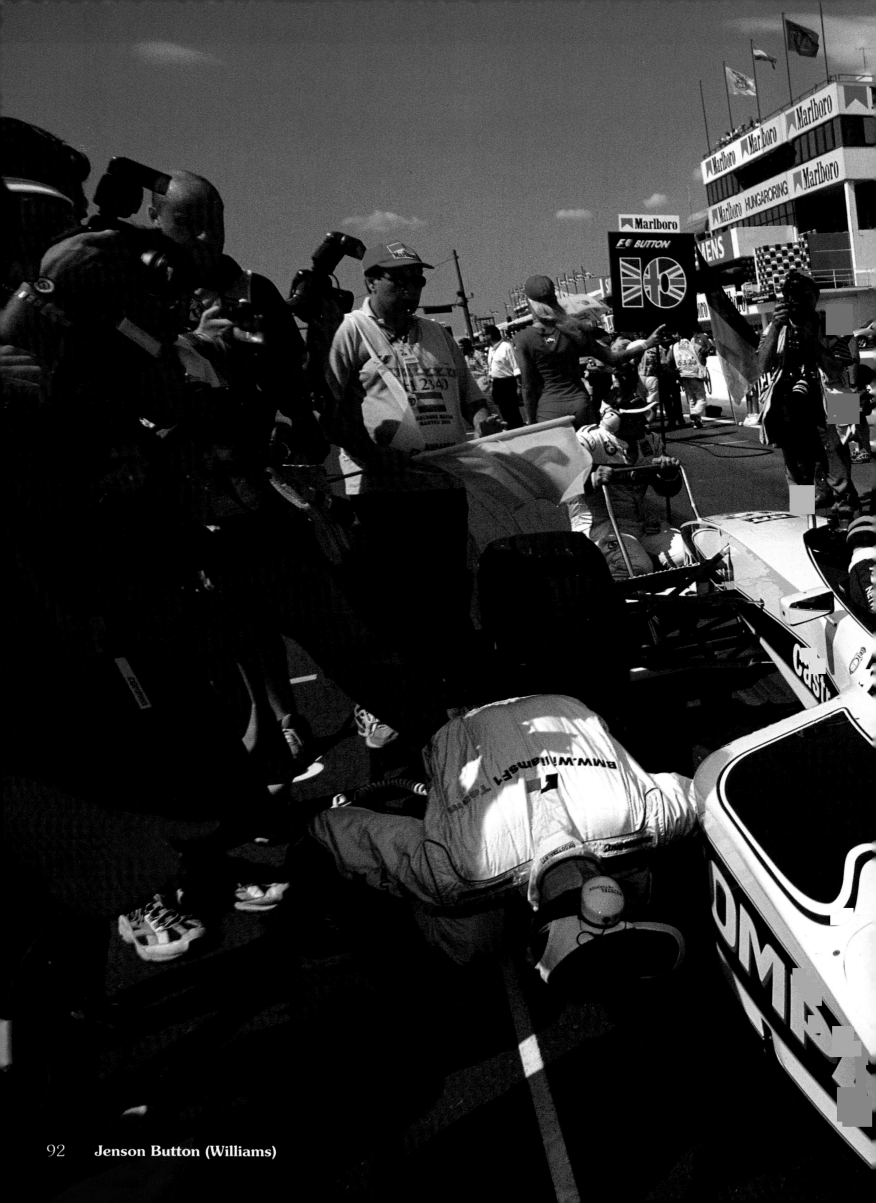

Jenson Button (Williams)

94   **Jos Verstappen (Arrows)**

Mika Hakkinen (McLaren)

98   **Heinz Harald Frentzen (Jordan)**

Monaco • J. Herbert (Jaguar) - M. Schumacher (Ferrari)

Jean Alesi (Prost)

G. Fisichella (Benetton) 125

PHOTOCOLORS - P. D'ALESSIO

PHOTOCOLORS - P. D'ALESSIO

PHOTOCOLORS - P. D'ALESSIO

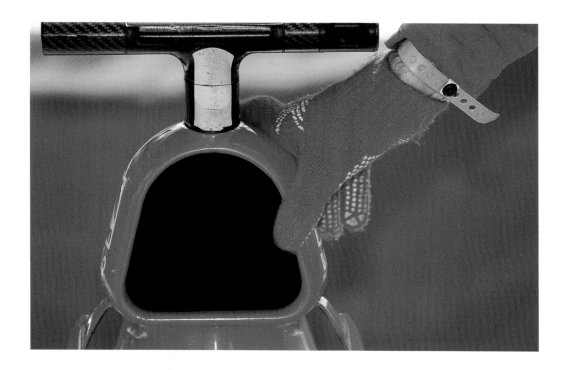

89
David Coulthard
(McLaren Mp4/15).

90/91
The traditional
end-of-race champagne
shower with drivers from
the three top teams:
McLaren, Williams
and Ferrari.

92/93
BMW made a low-profile
but highly successful
return to Formula One
with an incredibly
reliable engine.

94/95
Jos Verstappen
(Arrows A21).

96/97
Mika Hakkinen
(McLaren Mp4/15).

98/99
Heinz Harald Frentzen
(Jordan EJ10).

100/101
Three spectacular photos
of cars enveloped
in spray at the
Spa-Francorchamps circuit.

102/103
The Ferrari pits.

104
Johnny Herbert in
the crowded pit lane
at Monte Carlo.
It was a good GP
for Jaguar with Irvine
almost on the podium.

105
Giancarlo Fisichella
(Benetton B 200).

106/107
Alexander Wurz
(Benetton B 200).

108/109
Jean Alesi (Prost).
Jos Verstappen (Arrows).

110/111
Frentzen looks dejected
at his Jordan, which
has stopped out on
the Melbourne circuit
in the opening round of
the championship.

112/113
Eddie Irvine's race
in Brazil lasted just 20 laps.

114/115
Brazilian GP: Hakkinen,
in the photo, is ahead
of Schumacher but it wasn't
to last long because
the Finn stopped halfway
through the race with
engine failure.

116/117
Barrichello in action
in the Canadian GP where
Ferrari scored a superb 1-2.

118/119
Mika Salo
(Sauber C19).

Pag. 120
Jos Verstappen,
in pensive mood on
the time-keeping wall.

89
David Coulthard
(McLaren Mp4/15).

90/91
The traditional
end-of-race champagne
shower with drivers from
the three top teams:
McLaren, Williams
and Ferrari.

92/93
BMW made a low-profile
but highly successful
return to Formula One
with an incredibly
reliable engine.

94/95
Jos Verstappen
(Arrows A21).

96/97
Mika Hakkinen
(McLaren Mp4/15).

98/99
Heinz Harald Frentzen
(Jordan EJ10).

100/101
Three spectacular photos
of cars enveloped
in spray at the
Spa-Francorchamps circuit.

102/103
The Ferrari pits.

104
Johnny Herbert in
the crowded pit lane
at Monte Carlo.
It was a good GP
for Jaguar with Irvine
almost on the podium.

105
Giancarlo Fisichella
(Benetton B 200).

MILD SEVEN
Marconi

106/107
Alexander Wurz
(Benetton B 200).

108/109
Jean Alesi (Prost).
Jos Verstappen (Arrows).

110/111
Frentzen looks dejected
at his Jordan, which
has stopped out on
the Melbourne circuit
in the opening round of
the championship.

112/113
Eddie Irvine's race
in Brazil lasted just 20 laps.

114/115
Brazilian GP: Hakkinen,
in the photo, is ahead
of Schumacher but it wasn't
to last long because
the Finn stopped halfway
through the race with
engine failure.

116/117
Barrichello in action
in the Canadian GP where
Ferrari scored a superb 1-2.

118/119
Mika Salo
(Sauber C19).

Pag. 120
Jos Verstappen,
in pensive mood on
the time-keeping wall.

121
Pedro de la Rosa in action.

122/123
Jarno Trulli in action
at Monte Carlo.

124/125
Giancarlo Fisichella
at the Indianapolis circuit.
It was a bad weekend
for the Italian, and it
was made worse by an
argument with Benetton
boss Flavio Briatore,
who accused him
of scarce concentration.

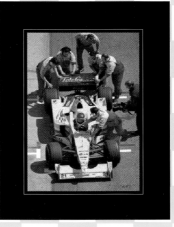

126/136
Formula 1 is not just speed and competition.
It is also the reign of colour, image and visual communication,
projected by means of mobile advertising
billboards called racing cars.
Visual communication is explicit and direct, but on
the other hand the technical element is jealously concealed.
The massive investments and interests at stake have transformed
the pit garage into an inaccessible, protected place where it
has become almost impossible to get near the cars
and discover their true secrets.
In these pages, we have tried to reveal a few of those secrets.

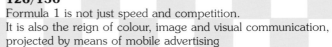

FORMULA 1 2000 : TECHNICAL FOCUS

by Paolo D'ALESSIO

Twenty-one long and never-ending years have passed since Ferrari's last Drivers' title, but in the end the boys in red did it. They succeeded in bringing back a title to Maranello that was starting to become a jinx. They managed to break a taboo that was bordering on a curse. And they did it in a record-breaking year.

Never before had a Ferrari won so many Grands Prix. Schumacher and Barrichello managed to beat a record that had stood since the days of the 500 F2 and Alberto Ascari's double title.

But it was no easy feat. Irrespective of the records, the victories and the joy at ending a 21-year drought, Ferrari's championship-winning season was anything but easy and the spectre of McLaren only faded away in the last couple of Grands Prix.

Ron Dennis's team, beaten on the racetrack, emerged from the 2000 season with its Anglo-German head held high... and with the knowledge that it has an exceptional car and nothing to envy Ferrari for.

But what about the others, we hear you ask...

As during the past three seasons, they stood out for their absence... or better still they tore each other apart for the final podium place. As a result, they had little to show for an expenditure of close to or in excess of 100 million dollars per year. But that's modern-day Formula 1 for you: you either take it or leave it...

This situation, on the basis of what we have seen in 2000, is not destined to last forever. Behind Ferrari and McLaren, the battle lines are being drawn and from next year onwards will probably include other teams, Williams and Honda above all.

The combination of BMW and Williams represented the third force in the world championship season that has just concluded, and the Anglo-German team finished the year on a high, with the knowledge that it can aim for its first Grand Prix victory right from the start of 2001.

On the other hand, one manufacturer that wasn't going anywhere fast in Formula 1 (apart from the door marked 'Exit'!) was Peugeot and it was Alain Prost who paid the consequences. The four-time world champion demonstrated, as if there were any need, that it's one thing to race in Formula 1 and another to run a Formula 1 team.

In 2001, but especially the year after, the candidates for the world title will have to keep an eye on Renault. The French company has an extraordinary record in Formula One and wants to play a leading role in the sport right from the start after a lengthy period away from the top category.

FERRARI F.1 2000

Even though at a first glance, last year's F399 and the current F1-2000
appear to be similar, there are a number of major differences between the two cars.
The nose is higher than the F399, tapers down at the front and is linked to the front
wing by means of two wide uprights. The design of the sides is also different.
On the F1-2000 the sidepods have a pronounced hump in the middle and get
smaller towards the outside. This configuration, along with the high exhausts
and the tapering of the protective structures on the sides of the cockpit,
helps to clean and speed up the airflow over the rear wing.
The higher nose has clearly influenced the shape of the chassis,
which is higher and more squared-off than the previous model.
The design of the front and rear suspension remains faithful
to the F399. The 049 evolution however is a completely
new version of the V10 engine, with the vee angle
increased from 80 degrees to 90 degrees.
As a result the unit is slightly wider,
but more compact and has a lower
centre of gravity.

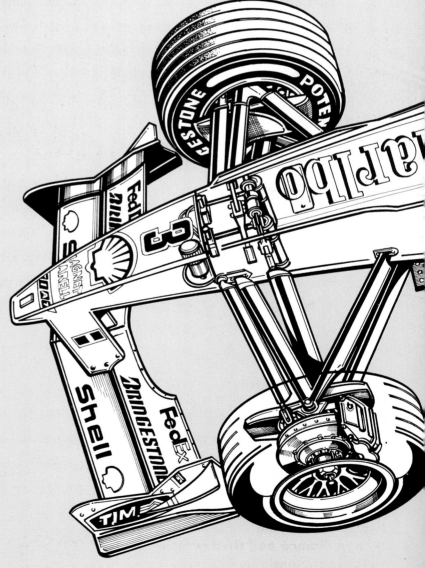

High exhausts, which were
considered to be a provisional
solution in 1998, have become a
common feature in the latest
generation of Ferrari cars.
For the record, 6 of the 11
teams entered for the 2000
world championship used
high exhausts.

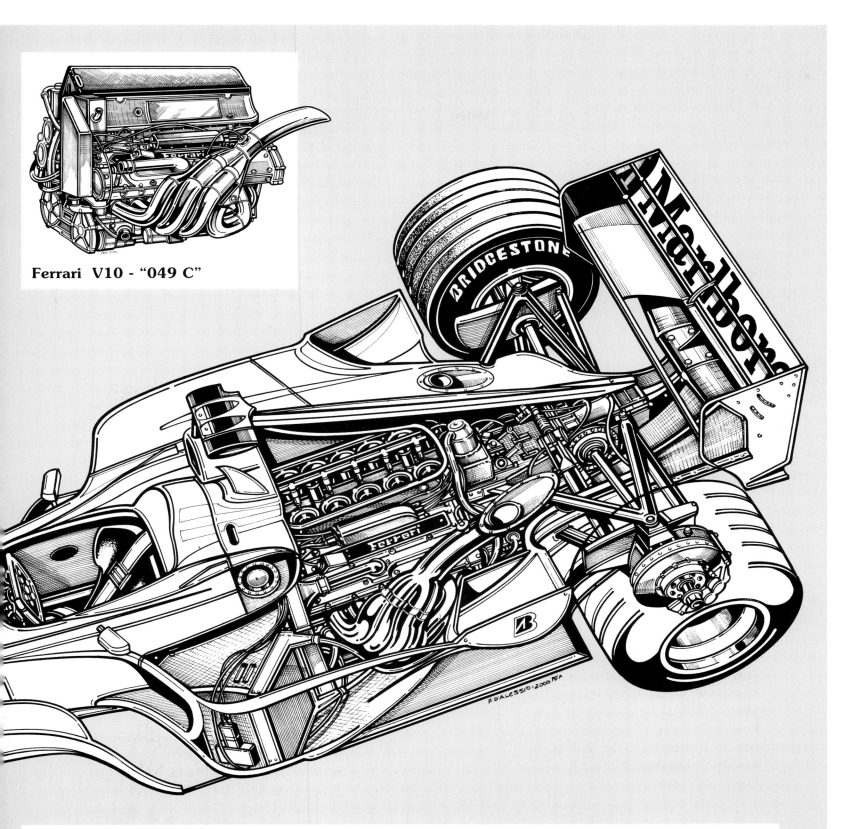

Ferrari V10 - "049 C"

Halfway through the season, Ferrari engineers introduced McLaren-style sidepod chimneys on the F1-2000. These original aerodynamic appendages allow cleaner airflow over the car and are extremely effective at drawing the hot air out of the sidepods. Ferrari tried them for the first time in France and they proved to be particularly useful on medium-slow circuits such as the Hungaroring.

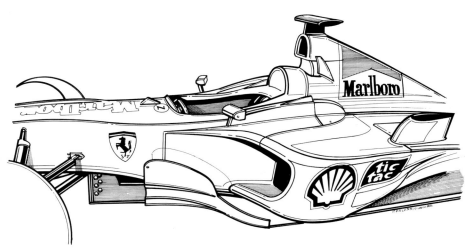

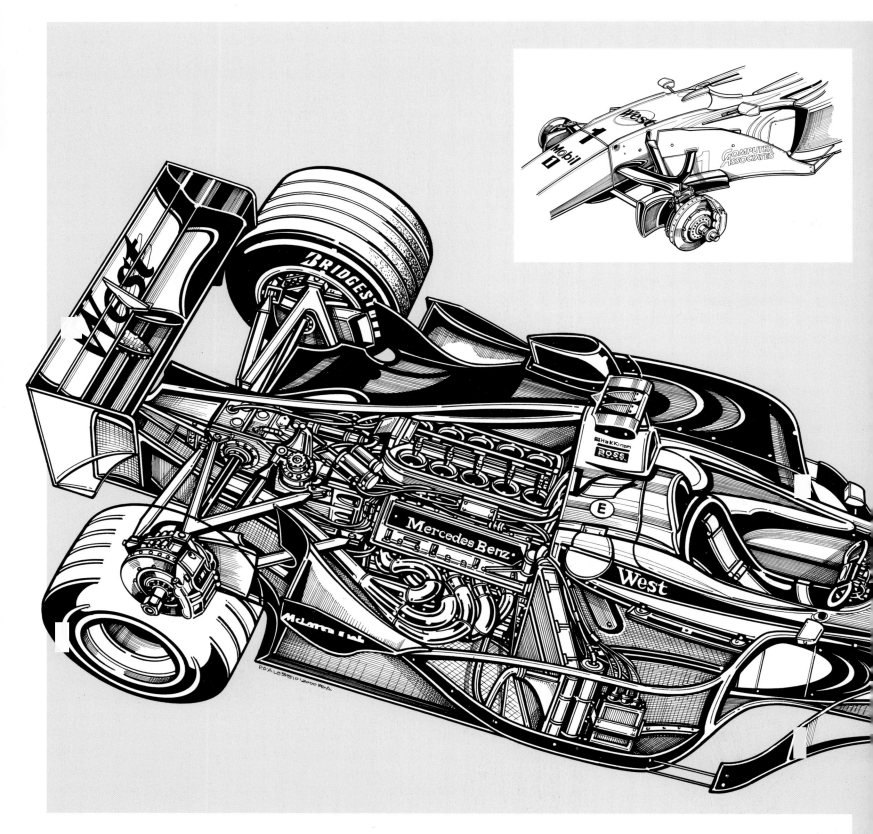

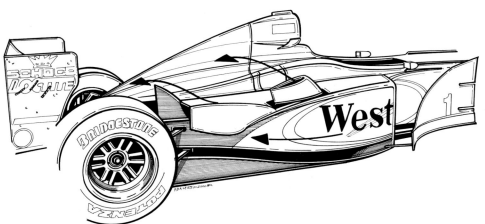

Right from its first shakedown tests, the McLaren MP4/15 adopted 'chimney' outlets on the sidepods. These unusual aerodynamic features have a dual function: they channel airflow over the rear wing and extract heat from the engine bay. Even though McLaren was the first to use them in 2000, they had been seen before in F1. In 1979 Shadow used something similar to extract the air flowing inside the Venturi ducts and increase downforce.

McLAREN MP4/15

Just like Ferrari, the McLaren MP4/15 was a logical evolution of the 1999 car.
Adrian Newey's project was based on the search for a lower centre of gravity,
excellent weight distribution and of course, an improvement in aerodynamics.
The low nose remained but the sidepod design was changed.
The sidepods on the MP4/15 are slightly shorter and more forward inclined.
In order to increase downforce at the rear, Newey also redesigned
the diffuser and the area around the cockpit. The engine cover and back
of the car are also different with a deeper Coke-bottle shape.
The MP4/15 presented a major change in the design of the rear suspension.
The torsion bar, which before was located on the outside
of the gearbox casing, is now placed in the middle of the rocker.
This more conventional layout allows suspension damper inclination
and compression ratio to be changed, depending
on the characteristics of the different circuits.

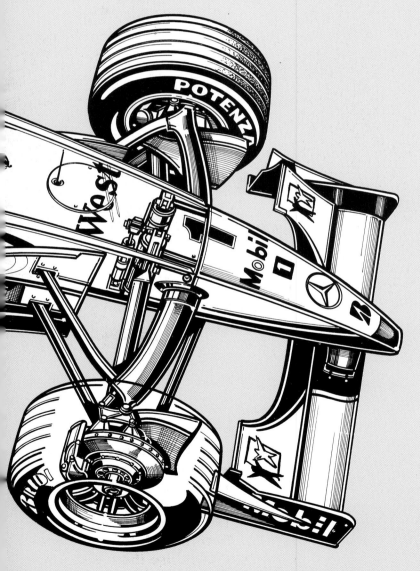

The nose on the MP4/15 appears
to be higher, but in fact it is exactly
the same shape and shorter.
Note the layout of the top suspension
wishbone, which became an
aerodynamic feature in order to
improve the channelling of airflow
towards the sidepods.
The front end was slightly
arched and also contained
the steering rods.

WILLIAMS FW 22

While Jordan and Jaguar were the disappointments of the season, the revelation of 2000 was BMW-Williams. Before the start of the season, doubts surrounded the return of the German giant to F1, in particular the 10-cylinder engine's poor reliability, excessive weight and fuel consumption. Doubts also surrounded the ability of the Williams engineering staff to repeat the glories of the past after the loss of Adrian Newey to McLaren. Instead nothing of the sort occurred and Ralf Schumacher even finished on the podium in the first race of the season, while team-mate Button, the real revelation on the driver front, scored points several times during the season. This was a sign that both the Germans, on the engineering side, and the Brits, with chassis structure and aerodynamics, had left nothing to chance.

On the FW22, Williams engineers retained many of the features seen on the 1999 car. The nose and chassis shape were virtually the same, while the sidepods were modified and are now slightly higher. The diffuser is similar in shape to its predecessor. Williams produced a new seven-speed gearbox for the FW22, while the oil tank was placed between the engine and the chassis, as opposed to between engine and gearbox.

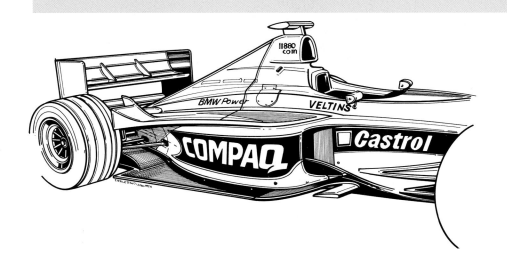

Another original detail of the BMW-Williams FW22 is the layout of the sidepods. Airflow entry into the pods is disturbed by a small Jordan-like wing, which divides air passing along the sides from the air flowing beneath the car. The shape of the flat front area is innovative with two small vertical fins.

The height of the Williams
nose is halfway between
the low level on the McLaren
and the high position
adopted by Ferrari.
The front of the
Anglo-German car is
less angular than 1999's
FW21 and does not have
the bump that characterised
the central part of the
old chassis.

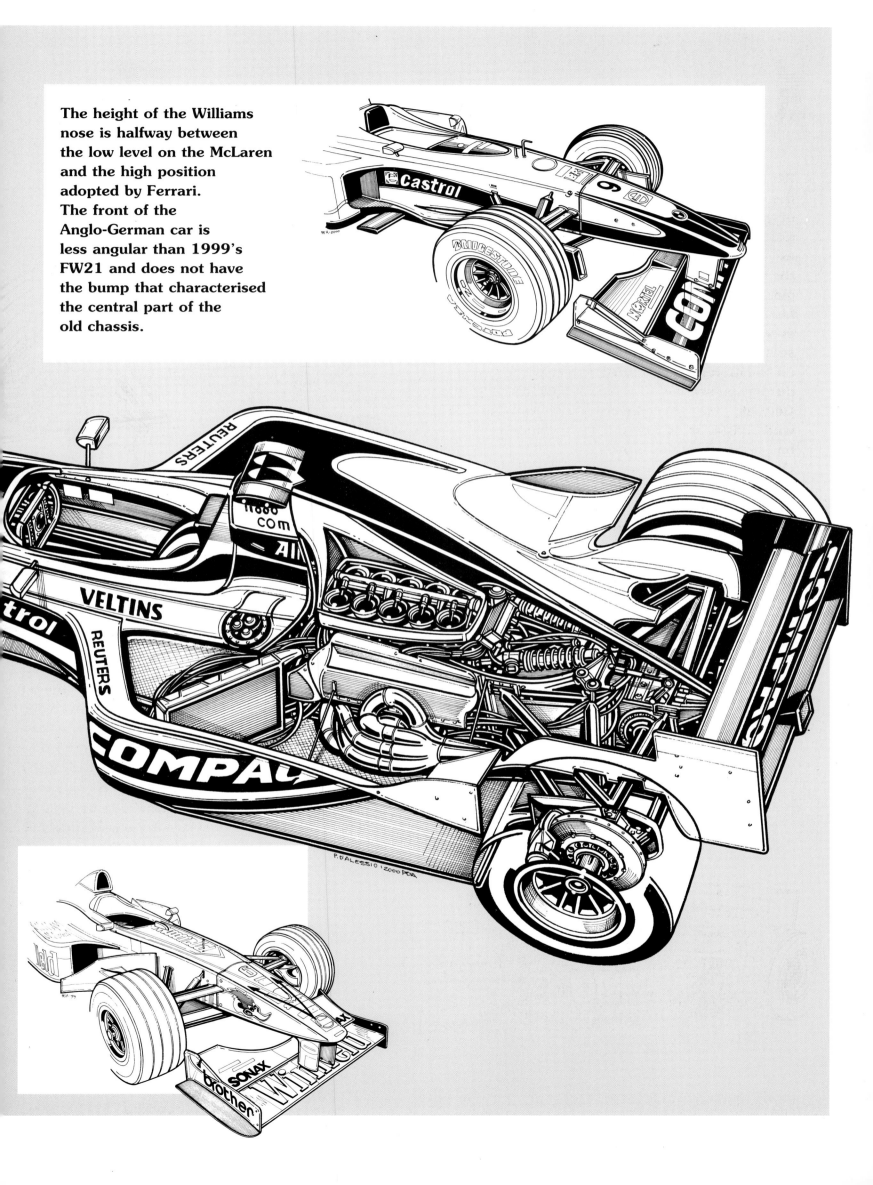

JORDAN EJ-10

The combination of Jordan and Mugen Honda was rated highly at the start of the season, and it was even thought that the Silverstone-based team could become the third force behind Ferrari and McLaren. Unfortunately it only appeared on the podium on rare occasions. There were two main reasons for this: the defection of Mike Gascoyne and the EJ10's problems. Eddie Jordan's right-hand man was more or less exonerated from his position at the start of the year, as soon as the news was out that he would be moving to Benetton in 2001. His replacements were unable to speed up the development of the 2000 car, which however had several basic faults, especially in the aerodynamics. Even though the engineers of the Anglo-Japanese team modified the design of the sidepods and the rear diffuser, the performances of Trulli and Frentzen showed little signs of improvement, evidence that the basic project had faults. Despite the lack of any good results on the track, Eddie Jordan did obtain one important victory when he succeeded in obtaining an official Honda engine deal for 2001.

BAR 002

The errors made in 1999 forced Reynard engineers to come up with a decidedly more competitive car than the first BAR. Like all his British colleagues, Malcolm Oastler, technical designer for the 002 project, was inspired by the 1999 McLaren-Mercedes MP4/14, which was the best car of last year. The similarity between the McLaren and the 2000 BAR can be seen in the design of the sidepods and the barge-boards. Nevertheless both Jacques Villeneuve and Ricardo Zonta complained about aerodynamic and structural problems on the 2000 car. One plus point was the performance of the powerful new Honda V10 engine, which could become one of the best on the grid in 2001. However, another negative note in BAR's season was the lack of any real reliability. Things went a lot better than 1999's disastrous debut, but Craig Pollock's team will surely have to improve in this area if it wishes to challenge Ferrari and McLaren.

After a couple of low-key seasons, Benetton again started to hit the headlines, more in view of 2001-2002 than its results in 2000. The reason was simple. After 15 years in F1, the Benetton family decided to quit and hand over control of the team. In came Renault, but in particular Flavio Briatore, the man who made the Anglo-Italian team great in 1994-1995 with three world titles. At the time, Michael Schumacher was in the Benetton cockpit. In 2001 the task of restoring honour to Benetton will be the responsibility of Italy's Giancarlo Fisichella and Jenson Button, the rising star of British motorsport. The first results of the Briatore cure could already be seen throughout the 2000 season. Despite the B200's limits, the Benetton drivers often managed to get into the points, inverting the negative trend that had begun a couple of seasons back. The real quantum leap in quality however should come in 2001, with the arrival of Mike Gascoyne and a brand-new Renault V10 engine.

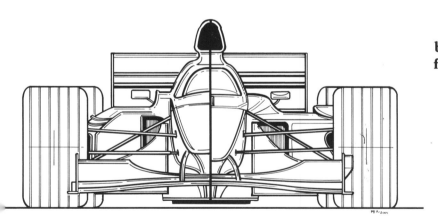

Defeat had been in the air for a couple of years and it finally arrived in 2000. Another troubled season, various misunderstandings between partners and a never-ending series of engine failures eventually convinced Peugeot to pull the plug on Formula 1 and concentrate on world rallying. It was an inevitable but disastrous decision for Alain Prost. After two disappointing seasons in 1998 and 1999, better things had been expected for 'l'equipe bleu'. Despite a massive budget, an excellent engineering team, the experience of Alan Jenkins and part-time consultant John Barnard, Prost had an even worse season in 2000. It was difficult to put the finger on the main defects of the AP03 because Alesi and Heidfeld suffered problems in virtually every department. Reliability and aerodynamics were just two of the sectors in which the French car was not up to the job, but even structural defects were discovered, which meant that the chassis had to be revised after the first few rounds. In these circumstances, it was impossible for the team to fight for the top positions, because all efforts were concentrated on just getting the cars to the chequered flag. It just goes to show that a massive budget doesn't necessarily count for everything in modern-day Formula 1.

PROST AP03

JAGUAR R1

The biggest disappointment of the 2000 season was undoubtedly Jaguar. The passage of the team founded by Jackie Stewart to Ford, which entered it in the world championship under the Jaguar name, attracted considerable interest in the F1 world. Not only because it meant a return of a glorious name of the past to top-level motorsport competition, but also because with its massive budget bankrolled by Detroit, Jaguar appeared to have all the right cards to succeed. Some insiders even went so far as to tip Jaguar for a race win in its debut season. Instead the Anglo-American team's first year concluded with a negative balance sheet and recriminations.

With the R1 model, Gary Anderson failed to improve the performance of the 1999 Stewart. Only on rare occasions did Irvine and Herbert succeed in emerging from the midfield, as they were hampered by the car's poor competitiveness and scarce reliability.

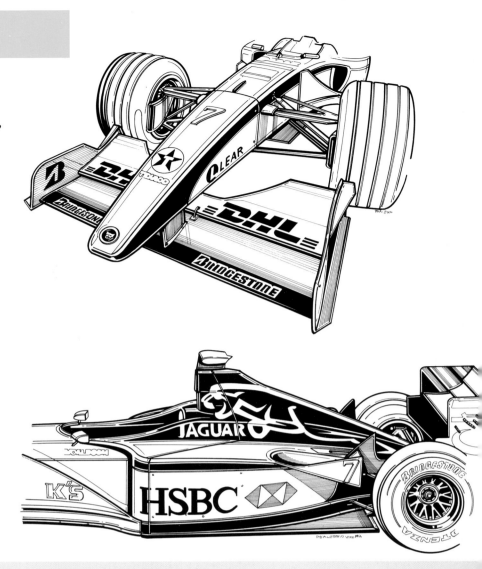

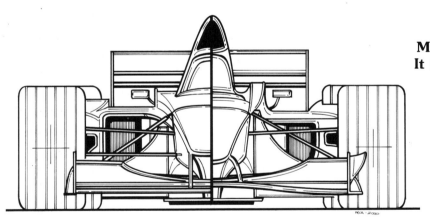

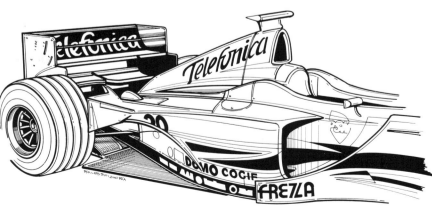

MINARDI M02

Despite celebrating its 250th Grand Prix in 2000, Minardi continues to be the 'Cinderella' of Formula 1. It is the team with the friendliest atmosphere, but also the lowest budget, in the Formula 1 paddock. The Faenza-based outfit had a relatively decent championship and with a more powerful, updated engine, could have moved into the midfield positions on a number of occasions. Much of the credit must go once again to Gustav Brunner, one of the best designers around. The Austrian made a clean break with the past to create an innovative Minardi, especially from an aerodynamics point of view. The nose was lower and more pointed, the sides were more compact, the exhausts were higher and the central part of the car was more refined. Another interesting innovation proposed by Minardi during the year was a new, more compact all-titanium gearbox. On the other hand, the team's main problems were on the engine front. Despite investing resources in the development of the old Ford V10 engine, the Italian team was unable to make the progress that its bosses, Gabriele Rumi and Giancarlo Minardi, had hoped for. It wasn't surprising however because the engines were a lot heavier and 100 bhp less powerful than those of its rivals. At this point, all expectations lie with the arrival of Supertec engines in 2001.

After a disastrous 1999 season and the departure of John Barnard, few people were prepared to bet on Arrows this year. Instead the Leafield-based team was one of the revelations of the season, with excellent prospects for the future. The credit for this resurrection goes to the A21 car and Tom Walkinshaw's technical staff who designed it. In particular, aerodynamics engineer Eghbal Hamidy, who designed a relatively simple but efficient car that was easy to set up and quick in straightline speed. The most original element of the entire project was the return of pull-rod front suspension. This design, which was in fashion in the 1980s, was dusted off by the Iranian engineer for aerodynamic reasons. The British team's season could have been even more positive had Verstappen's and de la Rosa's cars not been sidelined by a calamitous series of engine failures. Walkinshaw hopes to overcome the problem in 2001 when his cars will be exclusively equipped with AMT (Asian Motor Technology) engines from the company that bought out the entire Peugeot structure, including engines, premises and personnel.

ARROWS A21

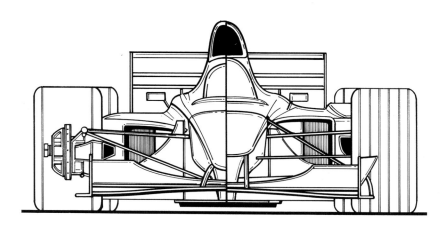

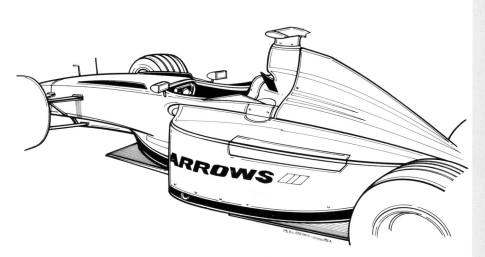

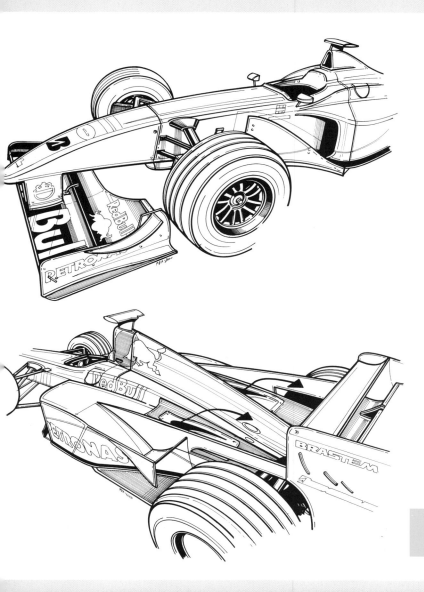

In 2000, the Swiss team again demonstrated that it was a solid midfield contender. This was quite a good result for a team without a factory engine (the 10-cylinder Petronas units are last year's Ferrari 048 engines) or a big budget. In the case of Sauber, the results were due to the C19, an unrefined but basically solid car. Even though the differences between the C19 and last year's C18 appeared to be minimal, Hinwill engineers revised every detail of the car, and succeeded in getting the weight down considerably. For example, the C19's nose was flatter and the front and rear wings and sidepods were totally revised.

SAUBER C19

Fifty years ago, on May 21st 1950, Ferrari made its debut in Formula 1. Those early days are a long time ago now: 50 seasons, 50 exhausting world championships have passed by with the constant presence of the Maranello manufacturer. This presence has transformed the scarlet-red cars into a sort of living icon of motorsport. Ferrari embodies Formula 1 itself, because without Ferrari Formula 1 would just not be the same, and without Formula 1, neither would Ferrari. It does not matter if the Prancing Horse cars win or lose, or if their rivals are more or less competitive on the track, because the legend will always shine through. In fact, the legend has always continued to shine through time, through periods of ups and downs, through controversy, adversity and defeat. Because let's face it, Ferrari is always Ferrari.

Ferrari can be forgiven for everything... almost everything. Even when the results are poor, a scapegoat can always be found. Depending on circumstances, the scapegoat can range from the malicious and meddling press, to designers who are not always up to the situation, from drivers who criticise, to sporting directors who are not always capable of doing the job. Ferrari in itself is never at fault. Managers, drivers, sporting directors, engineers, PR managers all come and go, but Ferrari is untouchable. It is accepted, like a dogma. It remains the same, always. But what is it that makes Ferrari unique? The fact that it is the only team that has taken part in every edition of the world championship? Yes, but that's not all. In its 50-year history, Ferrari has always accepted the challenge. It has never backed away from taking on small assemblers or major manufacturers. The Ferrari legend is a slightly anachronistic but original way of taking part in motorsport. When the word Ferrari is mentioned, it means everything. Chassis, engine, gearbox, bodywork and components. A middleman rapport with another manufacturer does not form part of Ferrari history. It does not exist in its DNA. Even though this might mean sacrifice, money down the drain and world titles lost.

It is of no importance. Ferrari is Ferrari and will always be so. Just imagine a brunette Marilyn Monroe or a bespectacled Mona Lisa! Unthinkable...

FERRARI F.1

PHOTOCOLOR - P. D'ALESSIO

1950 - 2000

1951 - FERRARI 375

1952/53 - FERRARI 500 F2

1954 - FERRARI 625

1954 - FERRARI 553

1956 - LANCIA - FERRARI D50

1958 - FERRARI DINO 246

1961 - FERRARI 156

1964 - FERRARI 158

1967 - FERRARI 312

1968 - FERRARI 312

1970 - FERRARI 312 B

1971/73 - FERRARI 312 B2

1973 - FERRARI 312 B3

1974 - FERRARI 312 B3/74

1975 - FERRARI 312 T

1976/78 - FERRARI 312 T2

1978 - FERRARI 312 T3

1979 - FERRARI 312 T4

1981 - FERRARI 126 C

1982 - FERRARI 126 C2

1983 - FERRARI 126 C2/B

1983 - FERRARI 126 C3

1984 - FERRARI 126 C4

1985 - FERRARI 156/85

1987/88 - FERRARI F1 87

1989 - FERRARI F1 89

1990 - FERRARI F1 90

1991 - FERRARI F1 91

1993 - FERRARI F1 93

1994 - FERRARI F1 412 T1

1995 - FERRARI F1 412 T2

1996 - FERRARI F1 310

1997 - FERRARI F1 310 B

1998 - FERRARI F300

1999 - FERRARI F399

2000 - FERRARI F1 2000

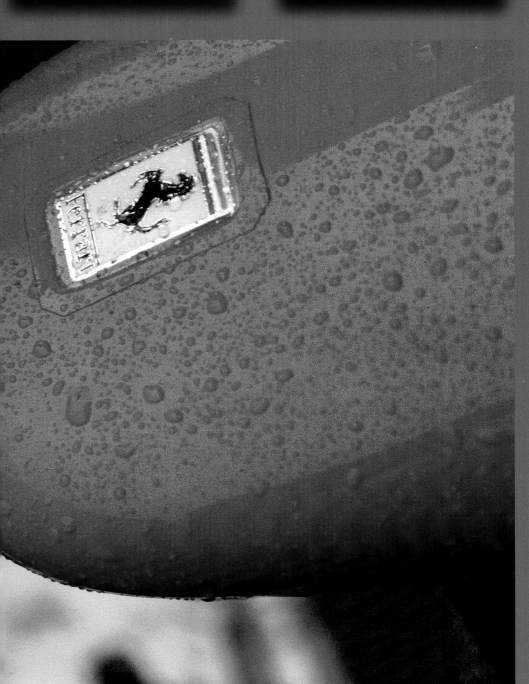

PHOTOCOLORS - P. D'ALESSIO

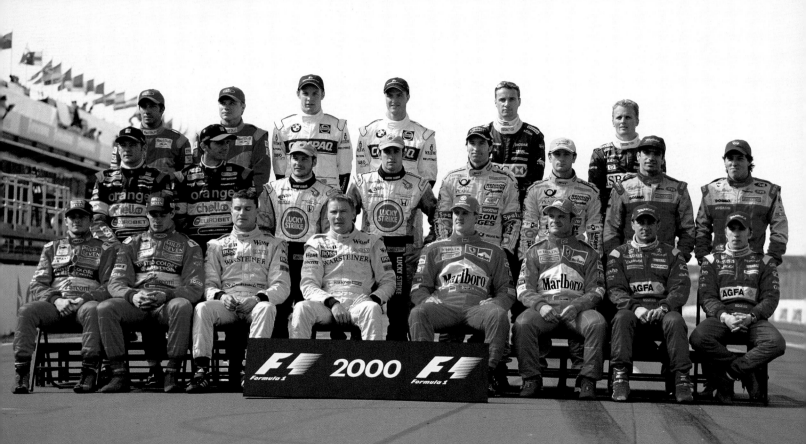

	1°	2°	3°
'90	N. Piquet	N. Mansell	A. Prost
'91	A. Senna	N. Mansell	G. Berger
'92	G. Berger	M. Schumacher	M. Brundle
'93	A. Senna	A. Prost	D. Hill
'94	N. Mansell	G. Berger	M. Brundle
'95	D. Hill	O. Panis	G. Morbidelli
'96	D. Hill	J. Villeneuve	E. Irvine
'97	D. Coulthard	M. Schumacher	M. Hakkinen
'98	M. Hakkinen	D. Coulthard	H.H. Frentzen
'99	E. Irvine	H.H. Frentzen	R. Schumacher

Australian GP

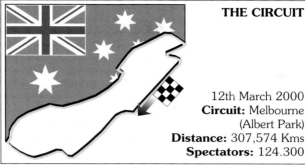

THE CIRCUIT

12th March 2000
Circuit: Melbourne (Albert Park)
Distance: 307,574 Kms
Spectators: 124.300

STARTING GRID

M. HAKKINEN McLAREN
1'30"556 (210,818)

D. COULTHARD McLAREN
1'30"910 (209,997)
1

M. SCHUMACHER FERRARI
1'31"075 (209,616)

R. BARRICHELLO FERRARI
1'31"102 (209,554)
2

H.H. FRENTZEN JORDAN
1'31"359 (208,965)

J. TRULLI JORDAN
1'31"504 (208,634)
3

E. IRVINE JAGUAR
1'31"514 (208,611)

J. VILLENEUVE BAR
1'31"968 (207,581)
4

G. FISICHELLA BENETTON
1'31"992 (207,527)

M. SALO SAUBER
1'32"018 (207,468)
5

R. SCHUMACHER WILLIAMS
1'32"220 (207,014)

P. DE LA ROSA ARROWS
1'32"323 (206,783)
6

J. VERSTAPPEN ARROWS
1'32"477 (206,438)

A. WURZ BENETTON
1'32"775 (205,775)
7

N. HEIDFELD PROST
1'33"024 (205,224)

R. ZONTA BAR
1'33"117 (205,019)
8

J. ALESI PROST
1'33"197 (204,844)

M. GENE' MINARDI
1'33"261 (204,703)
9

P. DINIZ SAUBER
1'33"378 (204,446)

J. HERBERT JAGUAR
1'33"638 (203,879)
10

J. BUTTON WILLIAMS
1'33"828 (203,466)

G. MAZZACANE MINARDI
1'34"705 (201,582)
11

Welcome back Formula One!

Saturday qualifying at Melbourne seemed to be an exact continuation of where the 1999 season had left off. Two McLarens were on the front row of the grid, with two Ferraris behind. But the illusion didn't last long, because twenty minutes into the race the two 'Silver Arrows' came to a stop with engine problems and Schumacher took the lead. The German would only hand it over to his team-mate Barrichello, making his debut in the Italian car, for a few hundred metres. On the pit-wall, Ron Dennis watched with amazement and disappointment as his two cars retired and even Hakkinen shook his head, repeating: 'we knew it wouldn't finish the race'.
It was a harsh lesson for Mercedes and its brand-new, ultra-light but very fragile engine. One overjoyed driver was 'rookie' Jenson Button who earned the plaudits of fans, journalists and his BMW-Williams team. Despite starting from the final row of the grid, he rocketed away at the start, overtaking five cars almost immediately. Button then retired a few laps from the end while in sixth place.
Ferrari, with a 16-point lead over McLaren, couldn't have asked for a better start to the championship. Schumacher won and Barrichello got onto the podium in his debut race, setting fastest lap as well.

HIGHLIGHTS

• Jos Verstappen recorded a top speed of 302 kph during the race in his Arrows.

• Jacques Villeneuve in 4th and Ricardo Zonta in 6th scored the first points for the BAR-Honda team.

• The 2000 'rookies' were 20 year-old British driver Jenson Button (Williams), 23 year-old German Nick Heidfeld (Prost) and 25 year-old Gaston Mazzacane (Minardi) from Argentina.

• It was a disastrous start to the championship for Jaguar-Ford. Johnny Herbert cooked his clutch at the start while Eddie Irvine spun to avoid de la Rosa on lap 6 and retired.

RESULTS

	DRIVER	CAR	KPH	GAP
1	M. Schumacher	Ferrari	196,254	-
2	R. Barrichello	Ferrari	195,858	11"415
3	R. Schumacher	Williams	195,561	20"009
4	J. Villeneuve	BAR	194,720	44"447
5	G. Fisichella	Benetton	194,696	45"165
6	R. Zonta	BAR	194,651	46"468
7	A. Wurz	Benetton	194,636	46"915
8	M. Genè	Minardi	190,472	1 lap
9	N. Heidfeld	Prost	189,215	2 laps

Mika Salo, sixth at the flag, was disqualified for an illegal front wing on his Sauber.

RETIREMENTS

DRIVER	CAR	LAP
J. Herbert	Jaguar	1
E. Irvine	Jaguar	6
P. De La Rosa	Arrows	6
D. Coulthard	McLaren	11
J. Verstappen	Arrows	16
M. Hakkinen	McLaren	18
J. Alesi	Prost	27
J. Trulli	Jordan	35
H.H. Frentzen	Jordan	39
G. Mazzacane	Minardi	40
P. Diniz	Sauber	41
J. Button	Williams	46

Australian GP | Brazilian GP | San Marino GP | British GP | Spanish GP | European GP | Monaco GP | Canadian GP | French GP | Austrian GP | German GP | Hungarian GP | Belgian GP | Italian GP | United States GP | Japanese GP | Malaysian GP

Schumacher 20

Barrichello 6

Hakkinen 0

Coulthard 0

It was another bad day for Irvine, who spun into the wall on lap 20. Positive return to F1 for Briatore, who saw Fisichella finish on the podium, and for BMW-Williams, but you wouldn't think so by looking at the expression on Patrick Head's face. Button rubs his eyes in disbelief at his 6th place and first-ever F1 points in his second race.

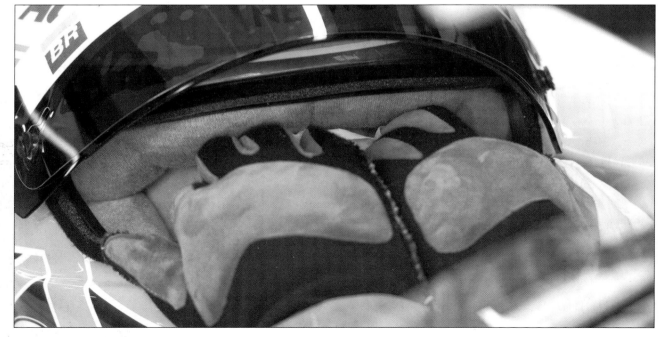

	1°	2°	3°
'90	A. Prost	G. Berger	A. Senna
'91	A. Senna	R. Patrese	G. Berger
'92	N. Mansell	R. Patrese	M. Schumacher
'93	A. Senna	D. Hill	M. Schumacher
'94	M. Schumacher	D. Hill	J. Alesi
'95	G. Berger	M. Hakkinen	J. Alesi
'96	D. Hill	J. Alesi	M. Schumacher
'97	J. Villeneuve	G. Berger	O. Panis
'98	M. Hakkinen	D. Coulthard	M. Schumacher
'99	M. Hakkinen	M. Schumacher	H.H. Frentzen

Brazilian GP

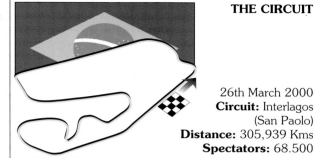

THE CIRCUIT

26th March 2000
Circuit: Interlagos
(San Paolo)
Distance: 305,939 Kms
Spectators: 68.500

STARTING GRID

M. HAKKINEN MCLAREN
1'14"111 (209,313)

(1) **D. COULTHARD** MCLAREN
1'14"285 (208,823)

M. SCHUMACHER FERRARI
1'14"508 (208,198)

(2) **R. BARRICHELLO** FERRARI
1'14"636 (207,841)

G. FISICHELLA BENETTON
1'15"375 (205,803)

(3) **E. IRVINE** JAGUAR
1'15"425 (205,667)

H.H. FRENTZEN JORDAN
1'15"455 (205,585)

(4) **R. ZONTA** BAR
1'15"484 (205,506)

J. BUTTON WILLIAMS
1'15"490 (205,489)

(5) **J. VILLENEUVE** BAR
1'15"515 (205,421)

R. SCHUMACHER WILLIAMS
1'15"561 (205,296)

(6) **J. TRULLI** JORDAN
1'15"627 (205,117)

A. WURZ BENETTON
1'15"664 (205,017)

(7) **J. VERSTAPPEN** ARROWS
1'15"704 (204,909)

J. ALESI PROST
1'15"715 (204,879)

(8) **P. DE LA ROSA** ARROWS
1'16"002 (204,105)

J. HERBERT JAGUAR
1'16"250 (203,441)

(9) **M. GENE'** MINARDI
1'16"380 (203,095)

N. HEIDFELD PROST
1'17"112 (201,167)

(10) **G. MAZZACANE** MINARDI
1'17"512 (200,129)

DINIZ AND SALO (BOTH SAUBER) DID NOT START FOLLOWING THE TEAM'S DECISION NOT TO TAKE PART IN THE BRAZILIAN GP ON SAFETY GROUNDS DUE TO REAR WING FAILURE IN QUALIFYING.

The Return of Briatore

Qualifying was a carbon copy of Australia, with two McLarens on the front row and two Ferraris behind. At the start, Mika and Michael get the better of their team-mates, but it was clear that it was going to be the Ferrari driver's day as the German outbraked the Finn at Senna's Esses at the end of lap 1. After a monotonous Australian GP, Formula One fans finally had something to shout about. The race was a succession of breath-taking moves and continuous attacks. Jos Verstappen, back behind the wheel in Australia after a long lay-off, drove an aggressive first lap to move up to 11th from 14th on the grid, and then passed both BARs, Frentzen and Fisichella to take third before tiredness got the better of him. While Barrichello stopped with hydraulics failure, Schumacher, whose Ferrari's oil pressure was failing, had to defend his lead from Coulthard. Third place went to Fisichella, who made it onto the podium in front of his newly-returned Benetton team boss, Flavio Briatore. Fisichella was then promoted to second after Coulthard's post-race disqualification for a front-wing infringement. Third went to Frentzen, followed by Trulli and the two BMW-Williams of Schumacher and the amazing Button.

HIGHLIGHTS

- A sixth place earned Jenson Button the first F1 points of his career.

- BMW-Williams were overjoyed at the performance of the German engine - 2 races and 3 times in the points (twice with Schumacher and once with Button).

- After rear-wing failure on both cars, Sauber decided to withdraw Salo and Diniz from the race.

- Jean Alesi also had a major fright when he was almost hit by a flying advertising hoarding in qualifying. Wind and poor circuit maintenance threatened to turn Saturday qualifying into tragedy.

RESULTS

	DRIVER	CAR	KPH	GAP
1	M. Schumacher	Ferrari	200,423	-
2	G. Fisichella	Benetton	198,979	39"898
3	H.H. Frentzen	Jordan	198,893	42"268
4	J. Trulli	Jordan	197,804	1'12"780
5	R. Schumacher	Williams	197,563	1 lap
6	J. Button	Williams	196,892	1 lap
7	J. Verstappen	Arrows	196,272	1 lap
8	P. De La Rosa	Arrows	195,775	1 lap
9	R. Zonta	BAR	194,770	2 lap
10	G. Mazzacane	Minardi	193,849	2 lap

D. Coulthard, second at the flag, was disqualified after the race.

RETIREMENTS

DRIVER	CAR	LAP
A. Wurz	Benetton	6
N. Heidfeld	Prost	9
J. Alesi	Prost	11
J. Villeneuve	BAR	16
E. Irvine	Jaguar	20
R. Barrichello	Ferrari	27
M. Hakkinen	McLaren	30
M. Gené	Minardi	31
J. Herbert	Jaguar	51

Australian GP   Brazilian GP   San Marino GP   British GP   Spanish GP   European GP   Monaco GP   Canadian GP   French GP   Austrian GP   German GP   Hungarian GP   Belgian GP   Italian GP   United States GP   Japanese GP   Malaysian GP

Schumacher 30

Barrichello 9

Hakkinen 6

Coulthard 4

After a fantastic weekend in Brazil, Imola was rather different for Jenson Button, who went out after five laps with another engine failure. Alongside: the spectacular BMW-Williams motorhome. Schumacher proved to be a worthy champion at Imola ... and quite an athlete! The German's jumps for joy accompany his every victory. In today's F1, everything is top-secret and cars, such as the Ferrari (right), are quickly covered to ward off prying eyes. A pit wall meeting involving Barrichello, Ross Brawn and Ferrari engineers.

	1°	2°	3°
'90	R. Patrese	G. Berger	A. Nannini
'91	A. Senna	G. Berger	J. Lehto
'92	N. Mansell	R. Patrese	A. Senna
'93	A. Prost	M. Schumacher	M. Brundell
'94	M. Schumacher	N. Larini	M. Hakkinen
'95	D. Hill	J. Alesi	G. Berger
'96	D. Hill	M. Schumacher	G. Berger
'97	H.H. Frentzen	M. Schumacher	E. Irvine
'98	D. Coulthard	M. Schumacher	E. Irvine
'99	M. Schumacher	D. Coulthard	R. Barrichello

San Marino GP

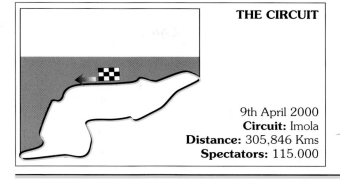

THE CIRCUIT

9th April 2000
Circuit: Imola
Distance: 305,846 Kms
Spectators: 115.000

STARTING GRID

M. Hakkinen McLaren
1'24"714 (209,632)

(1) M. Schumacher Ferrari
1'24"805 (209,407)

D. Coulthard McLaren
1'25"014 (208,893)

(2) R. Barrichello Ferrari
1'25"242 (208,334)

R. Schumacher Williams
1'25"871 (206,808)

(3) H.H. Frentzen Jordan
1'25"892 (206,757)

E. Irvine Jaguar
1'25"929 (206,668)

(4) J. Trulli Jordan
1'26"002 (206,493)

J. Villeneuve BAR
1'26"124 (206,200)

(5) P. Diniz Sauber
1'26"238 (205,928)

A. Wurz Benetton
1'26"281 (205,825)

(6) M. Salo Sauber
1'26"336 (205,694)

P. De La Rosa Arrows
1'26"349 (205,663)

(7) R. Zonta BAR
1'26"814 (204,561)

J. Alesi Prost
1'26"824 (204,538)

(8) J. Verstappen Arrows
1'26"845 (204,488)

J. Herbert Jaguar
1'27"051 (204,005)

(9) J. Button Williams
1'27"135 (203,808)

G. Fisichella Benetton
1'27"253 (203,532)

(10) G. Mazzacane Minardi
1'28"161 (201,436)

M. Gene' Minardi
1'28"333 (201,044)

(11) N. Heidfeld Prost
1'28"361 (200,980)

Ferrari Hat-Trick

This time, Michael Schumacher's third successive win was a victory for the Ferrari team, whose brilliant pit-stop strategy allowed the German champion to hold on to a one-second lead over the McLaren of Hakkinen at the chequered flag.

Three wins in three races for Schumacher, with the '99 World Champion way behind on 6 points, meant that Ferrari fans were already dreaming about a world title that had been missing from the Italian manufacturer's trophy-case for the past 20 years.

Coulthard was third and Barrichello fourth ahead of Villeneuve and Salo, who picked up a point for Sauber with a gutsy drive.

Jacques Villeneuve was again magnificent at the start, when the Canadian muscled his way into fifth at the first curve, after blasting past Irvine, Trulli, Ralf Schumacher and Frentzen from the fifth row.

It was a bad day for Williams with its two young drivers retiring with engine problems, while the Prost team fared little better, Alesi picking up his third retirement in three races.

HIGHLIGHTS

• Festivities at Imola for Scuderia Minardi, which notched up its 15th year of activity in Formula One after making its debut in Brazil on April 7th 1985; for Jacques Villeneuve, who celebrated his 29th birthday and for Irvine and Frentzen, who both reached the 100 Grands Prix mark.

• Ferrari have won four of the twenty Grands Prix held at Imola: twice with Schumacher (1999 and 2000) and once with Pironi (1982) and Tambay (1983).

• Jos Verstappen (Arrows) again recorded the top speed of the weekend, clocking 300 kph at Imola.

• Senna (1988, 1989 and 1991), Schumacher (1993, 1999 and 2000) and Prost (1984, 1986 and 1993) have scored the most wins at Imola, followed by Mansell (1987 and 1992) and Damon Hill (1995 and 1996).

RESULTS

	DRIVER	CAR	KPH	GAP
1	M. Schumacher	Ferrari	200,198	-
2	M. Hakkinen	McLaren	200,156	1"168
3	D. Coulthard	McLaren	198,359	51"008
4	R. Barrichello	Ferrari	197,000	1'29"276
5	J. Villeneuve	BAR	196,289	1 lap
6	M. Salo	Sauber	196,271	1 lap
7	E. Irvine	Jaguar	196,034	1 lap
8	P. Diniz	Sauber	195,891	1 lap
9	A. Wurz	Benetton	195,096	1 lap
10	J. Herbert	Jaguar	194,916	1 lap
11	G. Fisichella	Benetton	194,895	1 lap
12	R. Zonta	BAR	194,116	1 lap
13	G. Mazzacane	Minardi	190,889	2 laps
14	J. Verstappen	Arrows	190,328	3 laps
15	J. Trulli	Jordan	195,920	4 laps

RETIREMENTS

DRIVER	CAR	LAP
H.H. Frentzen	Jordan	4
M. Gené	Minardi	5
J. Button	Williams	5
N. Heidfeld	Prost	22
J. Alesi	Prost	25
R. Schumacher	Williams	45
P. De La Rosa	Arrows	49

Australian GP   Brazilian GP   San Marino GP   British GP   Spanish GP   European GP   Monaco GP   Canadian GP   French GP   Austrian GP   German GP   Hungarian GP   Belgian GP   Italian GP   United States GP   Japanese GP   Malaysian GP

Schumacher 34

Barrichello 9

Hakkinen 12

Coulthard 14

Appalling weather conditions blighted the British GP, flooding campsites and creating massive tailbacks, involving not only spectators but also team personnel. But the bad weather did not take away the smile from the faces of Ron Dennis and Norbert Haug after the McLaren 1-2. 'Rookie' of the year, Jenson Button was in the points yet again.

British GP

	1°	2°	3°
'90	A. Prost	T. Boutsen	A. Senna
'91	N. Mansell	G. Berger	A. Prost
'92	N. Mansell	R. Patrese	M. Brundle
'93	A. Prost	M. Schumacher	R. Patrese
'94	D. Hill	M. Schumacher	J. Alesi
'95	J. Herbert	J. Alesi	D. Coulthard
'96	J. Villeneuve	G. Berger	M. Hakkinen
'97	J. Villeneuve	J. Alesi	A. Wurz
'98	M. Schumacher	M. Hakkinen	E. Irvine
'99	D. Coulthard	E. Irvine	R. Schumacher

THE CIRCUIT

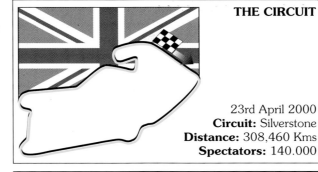

23rd April 2000
Circuit: Silverstone
Distance: 308,460 Kms
Spectators: 140.000

STARTING GRID

1
R. BARRICHELLO FERRARI
1'25"703 (215,950)

H.H. FRENTZEN JORDAN
1'25"706 (215,943)

2
M. HAKKINEN MCLAREN
1'25"741 (215,855)

D. COULTHARD MCLAREN
1'26"088 (214,985)

3
M. SCHUMACHER FERRARI
1'26"161 (214,803)

J. BUTTON WILLIAMS
1'26"733 (213,386)

4
R. SCHUMACHER WILLIAMS
1'26"786 (213,256)

J. VERSTAPPEN ARROWS
1'26"793 (213,238)

5
E. IRVINE JAGUAR
1'26"818 (213,177)

J. VILLENEUVE BAR
1'27"025 (212,670)

6
J. TRULLI JORDAN
1'27"164 (212,331)

G. FISICHELLA BENETTON
1'27"253 (212,114)

7
P. DINIZ SAUBER
1'27"301 (211,998)

J. HERBERT JAGUAR
1'27"461 (211,610)

8
J. ALESI PROST
1'27"559 (211,373)

R. ZONTA BAR
1'27"772 (210,860)

9
N. HEIDFELD PROST
1'27"806 (210,778)

M. SALO SAUBER
1'28"110 (210,051)

10
P. DE LA ROSA ARROWS
1'28"135 (209,991)

A. WURZ BENETTON
1'28"205 (209,825)

11
M. GENE' MINARDI
1'28"253 (209,711)

G. MAZZACANE MINARDI
1'29"174 (207,545)

McLaren back on form!

A win for Coulthard ahead of his team-mate Hakkinen with Schumacher third. These three made up the podium of the British GP, but the real protagonists of the weekend could be found elsewhere.

The rain might have upset the qualifying hour, but in difficult conditions, the lesser drivers often come to the front with courage and determination. For example, Rubens Barrichello set his first pole for Ferrari and the third of his career after Spa 1994 and Magny-Cours 1999.

Heinz-Harald Frentzen finally put the inconstant Jordan on the front row, Jenson Button was sixth quickest in qualifying and fifth at the finish and Jos Verstappen qualified eighth with a fast but fragile Arrows. Barrichello got the best start and looked good as he led the first 30 laps but falling hydraulic pressure cost him the lead and he retired five laps later.

Coulthard went on to win, with Hakkinen in second place, and the McLaren-Mercedes 1-2 restored some morale to the Anglo-German team after its early season problems.

HIGHLIGHTS

• McLaren scored its 36th 1-2 win in Britain, with Coulthard repeating his 1999 success for his second successive British GP victory.

• At Silverstone, Shell renewed its sponsorship deal with Ferrari until 2005.

• With just over one minute left until the end of qualifying, Jos Verstappen was in pole position. The last time Arrows was on pole was in 1981 at Long Beach with the Italian driver Riccardo Patrese.

RESULTS

	DRIVER	CAR	KPH	GAP
1	D. Coulthard	McLaren	208,266	-
2	M. Hakkinen	McLaren	208,208	1"477
3	M. Schumacher	Ferrari	207,490	19"917
4	R. Schumacher	Williams	206,664	41"312
5	J. Button	Williams	206,033	57"759
6	J. Trulli	Jordan	205,214	1'19"273
7	G. Fisichella	Benetton	204,672	1 lap
8	M. Salo	Sauber	203,839	1 lap
9	A. Wurz	Benetton	203,789	1 lap
10	J. Alesi	Prost	203,682	1 lap
11	P. Diniz	Sauber	203,654	1 lap
12	J. Herbert	Jaguar	203,605	1 lap
13	E. Irvine	Jaguar	203,492	1 lap
14	M. Gené	Minardi	203,104	1 lap
15	G. Mazzacane	Minardi	202,882	1 lap
16	J. Villeneuve	BAR	204,745	4 laps
17	H.H. Frentzen	Jordan	204,445	6 laps

RETIREMENTS

DRIVER	CAR	LAP
J. Verstappen	Arrows	20
P. De La Rosa	Arrows	25
R. Barrichello	Ferrari	35
R. Zonta	BAR	36
N. Heidfeld	Prost	51

Schumacher 36

Barrichello 13

Hakkinen 22

Coulthard 20

The Minardi team brought both of its cars to the finish - a good result in the home territory of its sponsor, Telefonica. Celebrations in the holding area immediately after McLaren's 1-2 win. Coulthard (left) is with his girlfriend Heidi. On lap 21 Jacques Villeneuve stopped out on the circuit with flames coming out of his engine.

	1°	2°	3°
'90	A. Prost	N. Mansell	A. Nannini
'91	N. Mansell	A. Prost	R. Patrese
'92	N. Mansell	M. Schumacher	J. Alesi
'93	A. Prost	A. Senna	M. Schumacher
'94	D. Hill	M. Schumacher	M. Brundell
'95	M. Schumacher	J. Herbert	G. Berger
'96	M. Schumacher	J. Alesi	J. Villeneuve
'97	J. Villeneuve	O. Panis	J. Alesi
'98	M. Hakkinen	D. Coulthard	M. Schumacher
'99	M. Hakkinen	D. Coulthard	M. Schumacher

Spanish GP

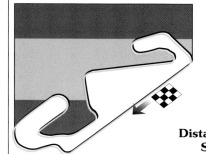

THE CIRCUIT

7th May 2000
Circuit: Barcellona
Distance: 307,450 Kms
Spectators: 79.000

STARTING GRID

M. SCHUMACHER FERRARI
1'20"974 (210,290)

1 **M. HAKKINEN** McLAREN
1'21"052 (210,087)

R. BARRICHELLO FERRARI
1'21"416 (209,148)

2 **D. COULTHARD** McLAREN
1'21"422 (209,133)

R. SCHUMACHER WILLIAMS
1'21"605 (208,664)

3 **J. VILLENEUVE** BAR
1'21"963 (207,752)

J. TRULLI JORDAN
1'22"006 (207,643)

4 **H.H. FRENTZEN** JORDAN
1'22"135 (207,317)

E. IRVINE JAGUAR
1'22"370 (206,726)

5 **J. BUTTON** WILLIAMS
1'22"385 (206,688)

J. VERSTAPPEN ARROWS
1'22"421 (206,598)

6 **M. SALO** SAUBER
1'22"443 (206,543)

G. FISICHELLA BENETTON
1'22"569 (206,228)

7 **J. HERBERT** JAGUAR
1'22"781 (205,699)

P. DINIZ SAUBER
1'22"841 (205,550)

8 **R. ZONTA** BAR
1'22"882 (205,449)

J. ALESI PROST
1'22"894 (205,419)

9 **A. WURZ** BENETTON
1'23"010 (205,132)

N. HEIDFELD PROST
1'23"033 (205,075)

10 **M. GENE'** MINARDI
1'23"486 (203,962)

G. MAZZACANE MINARDI
1'24"257 (202,096)

11 **P. DE LA ROSA** ARROWS
- (-)

Another McLaren 1-2!

The Spanish GP appeared to be going well for Ferrari when Schumacher claimed his first pole of the year. But it ended badly with Hakkinen and Coulthard on the podium, a furious battle between the Schumacher brothers and a Ferrari mechanic run over during a pit stop. Barrichello was the only positive note, the Brazilian finishing third after muscling his way past the battle between Michael and Ralf at the Sabadell Curve.
But the podium was devoid of celebrations as a sign of respect for the two LearJet pilots who died during a horrific place crash, from which Coulthard together with his girlfriend Heidi had emerged unscathed.
There was more disappointment for Jean Alesi, who retired on the second lap after a collision with de la Rosa. At 36 years of age and with 171 GPs behind him, Jean is F1's elder statesman and despite a lack of results, is one of the most popular drivers around.
It was another poor race for Jaguar, which saw both cars take the chequered flag, albeit down in 11th and 13th positions.

HIGHLIGHTS

- Imola KO! - a mechanic, Massimo Trebbi.
- Silverstone KO! - a photographer
- Spain KO! - chief mechanic, Nigel Stepney

Three GPs and three people run over by Schumacher! Will anyone insure him for next year's championship? Joking apart, Schumacher was not to blame for the most serious incident in Barcelona, because the mechanic in front of his car had given him the 'all clear' sign.

- It was Mika Hakkinen's third successive win at the Catalan circuit following the one in 1998 and 1999.

RESULTS

	DRIVER	CAR	KPH	GAP
1	M. Hakkinen	McLaren	196,405	-
2	D. Coulthard	McLaren	195,847	16"066
3	R. Barrichello	Ferrari	195,396	29"112
4	R. Schumacher	Williams	195,113	37"311
5	M. Schumacher	Ferrari	194,747	47"983
6	H.H. Frentzen	Jordan	193,591	1'21"925
7	M. Salo	Sauber	193,358	1 lap
8	R. Zonta	BAR	193,335	1 lap
9	G. Fisichella	Benetton	192,970	1 lap
10	A. Wurz	Benetton	192,290	1 lap
11	E. Irvine	Jaguar	192,255	1 lap
12	J. Trulli	Jordan	191,895	1 lap
13	J. Herbert	Jaguar	191,222	1 lap
14	M. Gené	Minardi	190,068	2 laps
15	G. Mazzacane	Minardi	189,039	2 laps
16	N. Heidfeld	Prost	186,686	3 laps
17	J. Button	Williams	193,985	4 laps

RETIREMENTS

DRIVER	CAR	LAP
P. Diniz	Sauber	0
P. De La Rosa	Arrows	1
J. Alesi	Prost	1
J. Villeneuve	BAR	21
J. Verstappen	Arrows	25

Australian GP · Brazilian GP · San Marino GP · British GP · Spanish GP · European GP · Monaco GP · Canadian GP · French GP · Austrian GP · German GP · Hungarian GP · Belgian GP · Italian GP · United States GP · Japanese GP · Malaysian GP

Schumacher 46

Barrichello 16

Hakkinen 28

Coulthard 24

Arrows' Spanish driver Pedro de la Rosa, here during his stop on lap 48, scored one point for sixth place. David Coulthard finished third, while Jean Alesi felt at home in the wet but could only finish ninth due to a stop-go penalty he picked up for speeding in the pit lane. But the winner was Michael Schumacher, here seen spraying the pit wall as he takes the chequered flag.

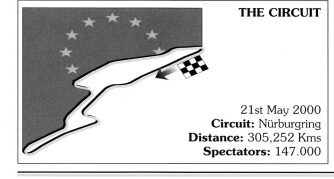

European GP

	1°	2°	3°
'90	-	-	-
'91	-	-	-
'92	-	-	-
'93	A. Senna	D. Hill	A. Prost
'94	M. Schumacher	D. Hill	M. Hakkinen
'95	M. Schumacher	J. Alesi	D. Coulthard
'96	J. Villeneuve	M. Schumacher	D. Coulthard
'97	M. Hakkinen	D. Coulthard	J. Villeneuve
'98	-	-	-
'99	J. Herbert	J. Trulli	R. Barrichello

THE CIRCUIT

21st May 2000
Circuit: Nürburgring
Distance: 305,252 Kms
Spectators: 147.000

STARTING GRID

1
D. Coulthard McLaren
1'17"529 (211,554)
M. Schumacher Ferrari
1'17"667 (211,178)

2
M. Hakkinen McLaren
1'17"785 (210,858)
R. Barrichello Ferrari
1'18"227 (209,667)

3
R. Schumacher Williams
1'18"515 (208,898)
J. Trulli Jordan
1'18"612 (208,640)

4
G. Fisichella Benetton
1'18"697 (208,415)
E. Irvine Jaguar
1'18"703 (208,399)

5
J. Villeneuve BAR
1'18"742 (208,295)
H.H. Frentzen Jordan
1'18"830 (208,063)

6
J. Button Williams
1'18"887 (207,913)
P. De La Rosa Arrows
1'19"024 (207,552)

7
J. Verstappen Arrows
1'19"190 (207,117)
A. Wurz Benetton
1'19"378 (206,627)

8
P. Diniz Sauber
1'19"422 (206,512)
J. Herbert Jaguar
1'19"638 (205,952)

9
J. Alesi Prost
1'19"651 (205,918)
R. Zonta BAR
1'19"766 (205,621)

10
M. Salo Sauber
1'19"814 (205,498)
M. Gene' Minardi
1'20"162 (204,606)

11
G. Mazzacane Minardi
1'21"015 (202,451)
N. Heidfeld Prost
Not Qualified

Schumacher Master of the Rain

Michael Schumacher's masterly win in the pouring rain took the Prancing Horse's total victory haul in 50 years of Grands Prix since its debut on May 21st 1950 at Monte Carlo to 150. In the wet the gap between the cars is reduced and talented drivers can finally show their true worth. This was the case with Jos Verstappen while he remained in the race and for his team-mate Pedro de la Rosa, who finished sixth, scoring Arrows' first point in this year's championship. It was also the case with Jean Alesi, who always goes well in the wet. Barrichello put in a fantastic performance but was penalised by Ferrari's decision to call him into the pits for three stops and at the flag an always-smiling Rubens was furious after missing out on third place. Schumacher stepped onto the podium with Hakkinen and Coulthard, who scored vital points for McLaren for the fourth successive race after the team's disastrous performances in Australia and Brazil. Despite Schumacher's win, Ferrari are starting to feel the pressure from McLaren.

HIGHLIGHTS

• First points for Arrows and Pedro de la Rosa with sixth place at the Nürburgring.

• Ferrari replaced Nigel Stepney, injured during Schumacher's stop in Spain, with Pietro Timpini. The Italian performed well in the high-pressure environment of the pit lane.

• Rumours surfaced at the Nürburgring that Benetton were trying to lure Jacques Villeneuve away from BAR for a massive sum of money.

RESULTS

	DRIVER	CAR	KPH	GAP
1	M. Schumacher	Ferrari	179,551	-
2	M. Hakkinen	McLaren	179,146	13"822
3	D. Coulthard	McLaren	176,656	1 lap
4	R. Barrichello	Ferrari	176,611	1 lap
5	G. Fisichella	Benetton	176,259	1 lap
6	P. De La Rosa	Arrows	175,807	1 lap
7	P. Diniz	Sauber	173,302	2 laps
8	G. Mazzacane	Minardi	172,934	2 laps
9	J. Alesi	Prost	171,955	2 laps
10	J. Button	Williams	173,747	5 laps
11	J. Herbert	Jaguar	173,929	6 laps
12	A. Wurz	Benetton	173,838	6 laps

RETIREMENTS

DRIVER	CAR	LAP
J. Trulli	Jordan	0
H.H. Frentzen	Jordan	2
M. Salo	Sauber	27
E. Irvine	Jaguar	29
J. Verstappen	Arrows	29
R. Schumacher	Williams	29
J. Villeneuve	BAR	46
M. Gené	Minardi	47
R. Zonta	BAR	51

Schumacher 46

Barrichello 22

Hakkinen 29

Coulthard 34

Two key features of Monte Carlo are the narrow pit-lane and the tight track, on which drivers have to slalom their way through first-gear turns, pavements and barriers. In the case of de la Rosa's Arrows, these do not allow any margin for error. Just look how close the Sauber of fifth-placed Mika Salo is to the barrier.

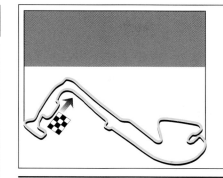

Monaco GP

THE CIRCUIT

4th June 2000
Circuit:
Montecarlo
Distance:
262,860 Kms
Spectators:
100.000

	1°	2°	3°
'90	A. Senna	J. Alesi	G. Berger
'91	A. Senna	N. Mansell	J. Alesi
'92	A. Senna	N. Mansell	R. Patrese
'93	A. Senna	D. Hill	J. Alesi
'94	M. Schumacher	M. Brundle	G. Berger
'95	M. Schumacher	D. Hill	G. Berger
'96	O. Panis	D. Coulthard	J. Herbert
'97	M. Schumacher	R. Barrichello	E. Irvine
'98	M. Hakkinen	G. Fisichella	E. Irvine
'99	M. Schumacher	E. Irvine	M. Hakkinen

STARTING GRID

M. SCHUMACHER FERRARI 1'19"475 (152,652)	1	**J. TRULLI** JORDAN 1'19"746 (152,133)
D. COULTHARD MCLAREN 1'19"888 (151,863)	2	**H.H. FRENTZEN** JORDAN 1'19"961 (151,724)
M. HAKKINEN MCLAREN 1'20"241 (151,195)	3	**R. BARRICHELLO** FERRARI 1'20"416 (150,865)
J. ALESI PROST 1'20"494 (150,719)	4	**G. FISICHELLA** BENETTON 1'20"703 (150,329)
R. SCHUMACHER WILLIAMS 1'20"742 (150,256)	5	**E. IRVINE** JAGUAR 1'20"743 (150,255)
J. HERBERT JAGUAR 1'20"792 (150,163)	6	**A. WURZ** BENETTON 1'20"871 (150,017)
M. SALO SAUBER 1'21"561 (148,748)	7	**J. BUTTON** WILLIAMS 1'21"605 (148,667)
J. VERSTAPPEN ARROWS 1'21"738 (148,425)	8	**P. DE LA ROSA** ARROWS 1'21"832 (148,255)
J. VILLENEUVE BAR 1'21"848 (148,226)	9	**N. HEIDFELD** PROST 1'22"017 (147,921)
P. DINIZ SAUBER 1'22"136 (147,706)	10	**R. ZONTA** BAR 1'22"324 (147,369)
M. GENE' MINARDI 1'23"721 (144,910)	11	**G. MAZZACANE** MINARDI 1'23"794 (144,784)

Giancarlo the Great!

Michael Schumacher set his second pole position of the season right at the end of the session after a fantastic split-second duel with Italian Jarno Trulli.

With a superb drive to seventh on the grid, Jean Alesi succeeded in hiding the faults of his troubled Prost. The race was full of upsets. Wurz started the ball rolling when he stalled on the grid after the first formation lap. On the restart, the luminous display board went haywire and caused the red flags to come out when the cars were already halfway round the lap. The race came to a stop anyway due to a snarl-up at the Grand Hairpin when Button tried to get past de la Rosa. Half an hour later the field finally got away and Michael Schumacher powered into the lead. He was to remain there until lap 53 out of 78 when the left lower rear suspension on his Ferrari failed at the beginning of the start/finish straight. Meanwhile more than half the field had been eliminated because of incidents (Wurz, Mazzacane, Diniz, Zonta and Ralf Schumacher) or due to typical Monaco GP wear and tear on gearboxes and suspensions. Coulthard found himself in the lead, followed by Barrichello and Fisichella, who drove a superb race on his home circuit. The same could be said for Mika Salo, fifth at the flag after defending his position for 10 laps from Mika Hakkinen.

HIGHLIGHTS

• After six races without any luck, Jaguar finally scored three points for fourth place thanks to Eddie Irvine. It was a tough race for the F1 'playboy', who climbed out of his car exhausted after his drinking system failed to work.

• Ralf Schumacher was involved in a nasty accident on lap 38 when his BMW-Williams went straight on at Ste Devote and into the barrier. The German cut his leg when the suspension arm went through the monocoque. He was taken to Princess Grace hospital, where the 7 cms cut was stitched up.

RESULTS

	DRIVER	CAR	KPH	GAP
1	D. Coulthard	McLaren	144,072	-
2	R. Barrichello	Ferrari	143,724	15"889
3	G. Fisichella	Benetton	143,667	18"522
4	E. Irvine	Jaguar	142,640	1'05"924
5	M. Salo	Sauber	142,322	1'20"775
6	M. Hakkinen	McLaren	142,125	1 lap
7	J. Villeneuve	BAR	141,367	1 lap
8	N. Heidfeld	Prost	140,693	1 lap
9	J. Herbert	Jaguar	138,794	2 laps
10	H.H. Frentzen	Jordan	143,690	8 laps

RETIREMENTS

DRIVER	CAR	LAP
P. De La Rosa	Arrows	0
J. Button	Williams	16
A. Wurz	Benetton	16
M. Gené	Minardi	21
G. Mazzacane	Minardi	22
J. Alesi	Prost	29
P. Diniz	Sauber	30
J. Trulli	Jordan	36
R. Schumacher	Williams	37
R. Zonta	BAR	48
M. Schumacher	Ferrari	55
J. Verstappen	Arrows	60

Schumacher 56

Barrichello 28

Hakkinen 32

Coulthard 34

Fisichella seems to have a special feeling with the Canadian GP, and the Italian scored his fourth successive podium, after the ones in 1997, 1998 and 1999. Jacques Villeneuve got off to a superb start, but then held up Barrichello and Hakkinen. Nick Heidfeld stopped out on the track with flames coming out of his Prost. Jos Verstappen was one of the stars in the wet.

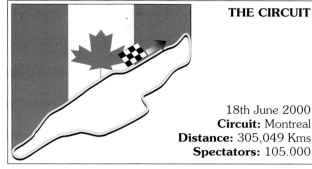

Canadian GP

THE CIRCUIT

18th June 2000
Circuit: Montreal
Distance: 305,049 Kms
Spectators: 105.000

	1°	2°	3°
'90	A. Senna	N. Piquet	N. Mansell
'91	N. Piquet	S. Modena	R. Patrese
'92	G. Berger	M. Schumacher	J. Alesi
'93	A. Prost	M. Schumacher	D. Hill
'94	M. Schumacher	D. Hill	J. Alesi
'95	J. Alesi	R. Barrichello	E. Irvine
'96	D. Hill	J. Villeneuve	J. Alesi
'97	M. Schumacher	J. Alesi	G. Fisichella
'98	M. Schumacher	G. Fisichella	E. Irvine
'99	M. Haakinen	G. Fisichella	E. Irvine

STARTING GRID

1
M. SCHUMACHER FERRARI
1'18"439 (202,904)
D. COULTHARD McLAREN
1'18"537 (202,651)

2
R. BARRICHELLO FERRARI
1'18"801 (201,972)
M. HAKKINEN McLAREN
1'18"985 (201,502)

3
H.H. FRENTZEN JORDAN
1'19"483 (200,239)
J. VILLENEUVE BAR
1'19"544 (200,085)

4
J. TRULLI JORDAN
1'19"581 (199,992)
R. ZONTA BAR
1'19"742 (199,589)

5
P. DE LA ROSA ARROWS
1'19"912 (199,164)
G. FISICHELLA BENETTON
1'19"932 (199,114)

6
J. HERBERT JAGUAR
1'19"954 (199,059)
R. SCHUMACHER WILLIAMS
1'20"073 (198,764)

7
J. VERSTAPPEN ARROWS
1'20"107 (198,679)
A. WURZ BENETTON
1'20"113 (198,664)

8
M. SALO SAUBER
1'20"445 (197,844)
E. IRVINE JAGUAR
1'20"500 (197,709)

9
J. ALESI PROST
1'20"512 (197,680)
J. BUTTON WILLIAMS
1'20"534 (197,626)

10
P. DINIZ SAUBER
1'20"692 (197,239)
M. GENE' MINARDI
1'21"058 (196,348)

11
N. HEIDFELD PROST
1'21"680 (194,853)
G. MAZZACANE MINARDI
1'22"091 (193,878)

Ferrari drink Canada Dry!

Five wins for Schumacher and three second places for Barrichello in eight races meant that things were looking good for Ferrari half-way through the season, with Coulthard 22 points behind.
On the circuit named after Gilles Villeneuve, Schumacher also set his third pole position of the year ahead of Coulthard, while Hakkinen was fourth, half a second down. In the race, Irvine stalled on the grid while Villeneuve blasted away as usual and passed Frentzen, Hakkinen and Barrichello in the space of a few metres. Schumacher kept the lead followed by Coulthard who had to pit for a stop-go penalty on lap 14. When the Scot came out, he had dropped to 10th. Halfway into the race, it began to rain, but then it stopped and there was chaos in the pits. On lap 43 Barrichello entered the pits to put on 'slicks', but two laps later he had to stop again to fit 'wets' because the rain was coming down in buckets. But Schumacher had just come into the pits and the Brazilian's tyres weren't ready, with the result that his stop lasted more than 20 seconds. Out on the track, Jos Verstappen was in superb form and as a result his Arrows was being followed by all the TV cameras.
The Dutchman took Ralf Schumacher, then Wurz and finally Trulli to finish fifth, scoring two vital points for Arrows. Despite his lengthy stop, Barrichello finished in second after catching Schumacher up towards the end, while Fisichella scored more points in third.

HIGHLIGHTS

• The 28 year-old Dutchman Jos Verstappen made his F1 debut in the 1994 Brazilian GP. He has been on the podium twice, in 1994 with Benetton, and has taken part in 64 GPs. He was the 'Driver of the Race' after moving up from 19th to 5th.

• McLaren notched up its 500th Grand Prix after making its debut at the 1966 Monaco GP.

• Fisichella stepped on to the Canadian GP podium for the fourth time in his career.

• Frentzen arrived in Canada directly from Indianapolis and described the new circuit as 'very fast'.

RESULTS

	DRIVER	CAR	KPH	GAP
1	M. Schumacher	Ferrari	180,850	-
2	R. Barrichello	Ferrari	180,845	"174
3	G. Fisichella	Benetton	180,393	15"365
4	M. Hakkinen	McLaren	180,299	18"561
5	J. Verstappen	Arrows	179,308	52"208
6	J. Trulli	Jordan	179,031	1'01"687
7	D. Coulthard	McLaren	179,016	1'02"216
8	R. Zonta	BAR	178,775	1'10"455
9	A. Wurz	Benetton	178,501	1'19"899
10	P. Diniz	Sauber	178,222	1'29"544
11	J. Button	Williams	178,193	1 lap
12	G. Mazzacane	Minardi	175,565	1 lap
13	E. Irvine	Jaguar	170,261	3 laps
14	R. Schumacher	Williams	180,569	5 laps
15	J. Villeneuve	BAR	180,513	5 laps
16	M. Gené	Minardi	179,158	5 laps

RETIREMENTS

DRIVER	CAR	LAP
J. Herbert	Jaguar	14
H.H. Frentzen	Jordan	32
N. Heidfeld	Prost	34
J. Alesi	Prost	38
M. Salo	Sauber	42
P. De La Rosa	Arrows	48

Schumacher 56

Barrichello 32

Hakkinen 38

Coulthard 44

Two McLaren drivers on the podium, with Barrichello the 'outsider' in 3rd place. Schumacher tried everything to contrast the McLaren domination and in particular to close the door on Coulthard, who responded with a hand gesture seen on television throughout the world. But the win went to Coulthard who can be seen here saluting the Magny-Cours public with a different kind of gesture. Note the damaged rear wing on Verstappen's Arrows.

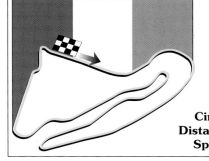

French GP

	1°	2°	3°
'90	A. Prost	I. Capelli	A. Senna
'91	N. Mansell	A. Prost	A. Senna
'92	N. Mansell	A. Prost	M. Brundle
'93	A. Prost	D. Hill	M. Schumacher
'94	M. Schumacher	D. Hill	G. Berger
'95	M. Schumacher	D. Hill	D. Coulthard
'96	D. Hill	J. Villeneuve	J. Alesi
'97	M. Schumacher	H.H. Frentzen	E. Irvine
'98	M. Schumacher	E. Irvine	M. Hakkinen
'99	H.H. Frentzen	M. Hakkinen	R. Barrichello

THE CIRCUIT

2nd July 2000
Circuit: Magny-Cours
Distance: 306,075 Kms
Spectators: 112.112

STARTING GRID

M. Schumacher Ferrari
1'15"632 (202,343)

(1) **D. Coulthard** McLaren
1'15"734 (202,070)

R. Barrichello Ferrari
1'16"047 (201,239)

(2) **M. Hakkinen** McLaren
1'16"050 (201,231)

R. Schumacher Williams
1'16"291 (200,595)

(3) **E. Irvine** Jaguar
1'16"399 (200,312)

J. Villeneuve BAR
1'16"653 (199,648)

(4) **H.H. Frentzen** Jordan
1'16"658 (199,635)

J. Trulli Jordan
1'16"669 (199,606)

(5) **J. Button** Williams
1'16"905 (198,994)

J. Herbert Jaguar
1'17"176 (198,295)

(6) **M. Salo** Sauber
1'17"223 (198,174)

P. De La Rosa Arrows
1'17"279 (198,031)

(7) **G. Fisichella** Benetton
1'17"317 (197,933)

P. Diniz Sauber
1'17"361 (197,821)

(8) **N. Heidfeld** Prost
1'17"374 (197,787)

A. Wurz Benetton
1'17"408 (197,700)

(9) **J. Alesi** Prost
1'17"569 (197,290)

R. Zonta BAR
1'17"668 (197,039)

(10) **J. Verstappen** Arrows
1'17"993 (196,218)

M. Gene' Minardi
1'18"130 (195,874)

(11) **G. Mazzacane** Minardi
1'18"302 (195,443)

Ferrari KO!

Is driving an F1 car that difficult? That's what millions of TV viewers must have been wondering when they saw Coulthard come alongside Schumacher at the Adelaide hairpin and wave one hand at the German in an internationally recognisable hand gesture while steering his McLaren round the corner with the other. It happened on lap 33 and was the Scot's first attempt to pass the Ferrari driver at the hairpin. He would succeed a few laps later, but almost risked crashing, when the two cars went round the hairpin side by side and touched, albeit slightly. The duel between the Scot and the German had begun during qualifying with Schumacher ahead of Coulthard by just a few hundredths of a second.
In the race, the pair blasted away together while Irvine, an excellent sixth quickest on the grid, got a bad start and dropped to 10th. Shortly after, Alesi passed his team-mate Heidfeld who tried to retake the Frenchman, risking an incident. There wasn't long to wait however as the young German, ten laps later, sent the veteran Frenchman into a spin.
Coulthard headed comfortably to the chequered flag, while Schumacher tried his best to hold off his hard-charging Finnish rival, Mika Hakkinen in the McLaren. Schumacher managed for 15 laps despite his Ferrari's clear inferiority, but two laps from the end his engine went and Hakkinen was runner-up with Barrichello again finishing on the podium in third.

HIGHLIGHTS

• First 'strike' in F1, when Peugeot engine personnel abstained from work for five minutes at the start of the Sunday morning warm-up in protest against Jean Alesi who had criticised the Peugeot engine the day before. It was another disastrous weekend for the all-French team, with disputes, a strike and its two drivers clashing out on the track.

* At Magny-Cours, McLaren confirmed its driver line-up for 2001. Hakkinen and Coulthard will be team-mates for a sixth successive year.

RESULTS

	DRIVER	CAR	KPH	GAP
1	D. Coulthard	McLaren	187,215	-
2	M. Hakkinen	McLaren	187,747	14"748
3	R. Barrichello	Ferrari	186,189	32"409
4	J. Villeneuve	BAR	185,284	1'01"322
5	R. Schumacher	Williams	185,201	1'03"981
6	J. Trulli	Jordan	184,840	1'15"605
7	H.H. Frentzen	Jordan	184,096	1 lap
8	J. Button	Williams	184,072	1 lap
9	G. Fisichella	Benetton	184,022	1 lap
10	M. Salo	Sauber	182,754	1 lap
11	P. Diniz	Sauber	182,300	1 lap
12	N. Heidfeld	Prost	182,265	1 lap
13	E. Irvine	Jaguar	182,000	2 laps
14	J. Alesi	Prost	180,366	2 laps
15	M. Gené	Minardi	180,351	2 laps

RETIREMENTS

DRIVER	CAR	LAP
R. Zonta	BAR	16
J. Herbert	Jaguar	20
J. Verstappen	Arrows	25
G. Mazzacane	Minardi	31
A. Wurz	Benetton	34
P. De La Rosa	Arrows	45
M. Schumacher	Ferrari	58

Schumacher 56

Barrichello 36

Hakkinen 48

Coulthard 50

The Austrian GP was a disaster for local driver Wurz, who was also criticised by his team manager Flavio Briatore. In ten races he has scored no points. The country might have changed, but the podium saw the same three drivers: the McLaren duo plus Barrichello. In the last two photos, Coulthard dominates the Austrian circuit from the top of the hill, while Mika dominates the media centre with his TV image during the press conference.

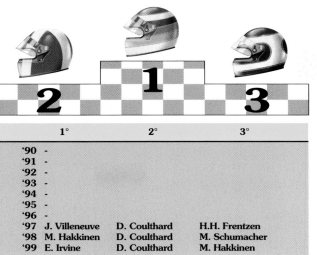

	1°	2°	3°
'90	-		
'91	-		
'92	-		
'93	-		
'94	-		
'95	-		
'96	-		
'97	J. Villeneuve	D. Coulthard	H.H. Frentzen
'98	M. Hakkinen	D. Coulthard	M. Schumacher
'99	E. Irvine	D. Coulthard	M. Hakkinen

Austrian GP

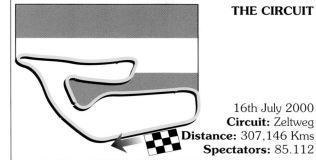

THE CIRCUIT

16th July 2000
Circuit: Zeltweg
Distance: 307,146 Kms
Spectators: 85.112

SPIELBERG 200

STARTING GRID

M. HAKKINEN McLAREN
1'10"410 (221,184)

① **D. COULTHARD** McLAREN
1'10"795 (219,982)

R. BARRICHELLO FERRARI
1'10"844 (219,829)

② **M. SCHUMACHER** FERRARI
1'11"046 (219,204)

J. TRULLI JORDAN
1'11"640 (217,387)

③ **R. ZONTA** BAR
1'11"647 (217,366)

J. VILLENEUVE BAR
1'11"649 (217,360)

④ **G. FISICHELLA** BENETTON
1'11"658 (217,332)

M. SALO SAUBER
1'11"761 (217,020)

⑤ **J. VERSTAPPEN** ARROWS
1'11"905 (216,586)

P. DINIZ SAUBER
1'11"931 (216,507)

⑥ **P. DE LA ROSA** ARROWS
1'11"978 (216,366)

N. HEIDFELD PROST
1'12"037 (216,189)

⑦ **A. WURZ** BENETTON
1'12"038 (216,186)

H.H. FRENTZEN JORDAN
1'12"043 (216,171)

⑧ **J. HERBERT** JAGUAR
1'12"238 (215,587)

J. ALESI PROST
1'12"304 (215,391)

⑨ **J. BUTTON** WILLIAMS
1'12"337 (215,292)

R. SCHUMACHER WILLIAMS
1'12"347 (215,263)

⑩ **M. GENE'** MINARDI
1'12"722 (214,153)

L. BURTI JAGUAR
1'12"822 (213,858)

⑪ **G. MAZZACANE** MINARDI
1'13"419 (212,119)

The Party's over!

This was the headline is an Italian motor-sport magazine after the Austrian GP. The reason? Two McLarens on the front row of the grid and a 1-2 victory for the Anglo-German team, with Mika taking his second win of the year.

The race was virtually over at the first curve, when Zonta crashed into a slow-starting Schumacher after just a few hundred metres. His Ferrari slewed round and was then hit by Trulli's Jordan. A few metres behind Schumacher's incident, Diniz's Sauber hit Fisichella and touched his team-mate Salo. Everyone thought that the race would be stopped because the German's Ferrari was resting on the outside kerb, but the race director thought otherwise and sent the safety car out while the marshals pushed the cars away.

The race saw an easy win for Hakkinen, who despite slowing towards the end, finished 12 seconds ahead of Coulthard and 30 seconds ahead of Barrichello, who picked up another third place. The real problem for Schumacher now was that Coulthard was just 6 points behind and Hakkinen 8 in the battle for the Drivers' title. In the Constructors' standings, McLaren would have been in the lead had it not been for the 10 points they lost when Hakkinen's McLaren was found to be missing a seal at the chequered flag.

HIGHLIGHTS

- In post-race scrutineering, Hakkinen's McLaren was found to have an FIA control seal missing from its electronic management system and the team were docked 10 points for Hakkinen's victory.

- Jaguar test-driver, 25 year-old Brazilian Luciano Burti, had to step in to replace Eddie Irvine on Saturday morning when the Ulsterman went down with stomach cramps the previous evening. Despite never having seen the Austrian circuit before, Burti ran a composed race without making any errors to finish 11th, two laps down on Hakkinen.

RESULTS

	DRIVER	CAR	KPH	GAP
1	M. Hakkinen	McLaren	208,792	-
2	D. Coulthard	McLaren	208,299	12"535
3	R. Barrichello	Ferrari	207,585	30"795
4	J. Villeneuve	BAR	204,974	1 lap
5	J. Button	Williams	204,838	1 lap
6	M. Salo	Sauber	204,802	1 lap
7	J. Herbert	Jaguar	204,784	1 lap
8	M. Gené	Minardi	204,448	1 lap
9	P. Diniz	Sauber	204,424	1 lap
10	A. Wurz	Benetton	204,394	1 lap
11	L. Burti	Jaguar	202,309	2 laps
12	G. Mazzacane	Minardi	199,968	3 laps

RETIREMENTS

DRIVER	CAR	LAP
G. Fisichella	Benetton	0
J. Trulli	Jordan	0
M. Schumacher	Ferrari	0
H.H. Frentzen	Jordan	4
J. Verstappen	Arrows	14
P. De La Rosa	Arrows	32
J. Alesi	Prost	41
N. Heidfeld	Prost	41
R. Schumacher	Williams	52
R. Zonta	BAR	58

Schumacher 56

Barrichello 46

Hakkinen 54

Coulthard 54

The photos alongside are entirely dedicated to Barrichello. Joy on the podium, tears during the national anthem, friendly congratulations from Hakkinen and a lap of honour after a fantastic race in the rain that flooded the circuit, as can be seen in the photo with the safety car.

German GP

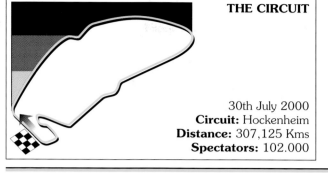

THE CIRCUIT

30th July 2000
Circuit: Hockenheim
Distance: 307,125 Kms
Spectators: 102.000

	1°	2°	3°
'90	A. Senna	A. Nannini	G. Berger
'91	N. Mansell	R. Patrese	J. Alesi
'92	N. Mansell	A. Senna	M. Schumacher
'93	A. Prost	M. Schumacher	M. Brundell
'94	G. Berger	O. Panis	E. Bernard
'95	M. Schumacher	D. Coulthard	G. Berger
'96	D. Hill	J. Alesi	J. Villeneuve
'97	G. Berger	M. Schumacher	M. Hakkinen
'98	M. Hakkinen	D. Coulthard	J. Villeneuve
'99	E. Irvine	M. Salo	H.H. Frentzen

STARTING GRID

D. COULTHARD MCLAREN
1'45"697 (232,457)

M. SCHUMACHER FERRARI
1'47"063 (229,491) — 1

G. FISICHELLA BENETTON
1'47"130 (229,348)

M. HAKKINEN MCLAREN
1'47"162 (229,279) — 2

P. DE LA ROSA ARROWS
1'47"786 (227,952)

J. TRULLI JORDAN
1'47"833 (227,852) — 3

A. WURZ BENETTON
1'48"037 (227,422)

J. HERBERT JAGUAR
1'48"078 (227,336) — 4

J. VILLENEUVE BAR
1'48"121 (227,245)

E. IRVINE JAGUAR
1'48"305 (226,859) — 5

J. VERSTAPPEN ARROWS
1'48"321 (226,826)

R. ZONTA BAR
1'48"665 (226,108) — 6

N. HEIDFELD PROST
1'48"690 (226,056)

R. SCHUMACHER WILLIAMS
1'48"841 (225,742) — 7

M. SALO SAUBER
1'49"204 (224,992)

J. BUTTON WILLIAMS
1'49"215 (224,969) — 8

H.H. FRENTZEN JORDAN
1'49"280 (224,835)

R. BARRICHELLO FERRARI
1'49"544 (224,293) — 9

P. DINIZ SAUBER
1'49"936 (223,494)

J. ALESI PROST
1'50"289 (222,778) — 10

G. MAZZACANE MINARDI
1'51"611 (220,140)

M. GENE' MINARDI
1'53"094 (217,253) — 11

First win for Barrichello!

Winning a Grand Prix for Ferrari has always been Rubens Barrichello's big dream. To win it by starting almost from the back of the grid and then driving on slick tyres in the wet must have been even more exciting. The Brazilian's last laps were followed with anxiety, not only by the Ferrari team in the pits, but also by millions of TV viewers. Ferrari and non-Ferrari fans alike must have appreciated the courage and determination of 'nice guy' Barrichello, who drove a great race but who was helped by a good dose of luck and the entry of the safety car.
In qualifying he hardly did any laps at all due to a problem on his Ferrari, and when he went out onto the track a few minutes before the end, heavy rain prevented him from qualifying any higher than 18th.
On the other hand, Schumacher's race, like the Austrian GP before, lasted just a few hundred metres. Boxed in by Hakkinen, Schumacher slowed and was hit by Fisichella, and both the German and the Italian were eliminated. Barrichello was meanwhile already starting his charge up the field. After 5 laps he had passed 12 cars and after 15 he was in third place.
The first surprise came halfway through the race, when a spectator jumped over the fence and walked onto the track with the cars speeding past at 300 kph. The safety car came out while the spectator was accompanied away by track authorities. On lap 32 out of 45 it began to rain heavily. Almost all drivers came in to change to 'wets' but Barrichello decided to risk staying out on 'slicks'. Despite being on 'wets', Hakkinen was unable to catch the Ferrari driver who took the chequered flag ahead of the Finn and Coulthard.

HIGHLIGHTS

- Jenson Button finished 4th, achieving his best-ever result and scoring points for the fourth time in 11 races.

- Benetton had to give up on signing Villeneuve, who decided to renew his contract with BAR for 2001, while Jordan confirmed Heinz-Harald Frentzen.

- Jarno Trulli lost out on an almost certain runner-up slot due to a stop-go penalty mistakenly awarded by the race stewards.

RESULTS

	DRIVER	CAR	KPH	GAP
1	R. Barrichello	Ferrari	215,340	-
2	M. Hakkinen	McLaren	215,028	7"452
3	D. Coulthard	McLaren	214,456	21"168
4	J. Button	Williams	214,393	22"685
5	M. Salo	Sauber	214,209	27"112
6	P. De La Rosa	Arrows	214,128	29"080
7	R. Schumacher	Williams	214,052	30"898
8	J. Villeneuve	BAR	213,365	47"537
9	J. Trulli	Jordan	213,226	50"901
10	E. Irvine	Jaguar	212,060	1'19"664
11	G. Mazzacane	Minardi	211,651	1'29"504
12	N. Heidfeld	Prost	213,919	5 laps

RETIREMENTS

DRIVER	CAR	LAP
G. Fisichella	Benetton	0
M. Schumacher	Ferrari	0
J. Herbert	Jaguar	12
J. Alesi	Prost	29
P. Diniz	Sauber	29
A. Wurz	Benetton	31
M. Gené	Minardi	33
R. Zonta	BAR	37
J. Verstappen	Arrows	39
H.H. Frentzen	Jordan	39

Schumacher 62

Barrichello 49

Hakkinen 64

Coulthard 58

The 'boss' and his 'boys': Bernie Ecclestone on the Hungaroring pit wall with the four protagonists of this year's championship. Ferrari president, Luca di Montezemolo, chats with Naomi Campbell, Flavio Briatore's companion, in the Ferrari motorhome. Hungarian GP winner Mika Hakkinen, who led from the first corner.

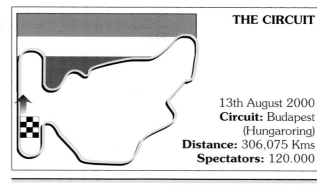

THE CIRCUIT

13th August 2000
Circuit: Budapest
(Hungaroring)
Distance: 306,075 Kms
Spectators: 120.000

	1°	2°	3°
'90	T. Boutsen	A. Senna	N. Piquet
'91	A. Senna	N. Mansell	R. Patrese
'92	A. Senna	N. Mansell	G. Berger
'93	D. Hill	R. Patrese	G. Berger
'94	M. Schumacher	D. Hill	J. Verstappen
'95	D. Hill	D. Coulthard	G. Berger
'96	J. Villeneuve	D. Hill	J. Alesi
'97	J. Villeneuve	D. Hill	J. Herbert
'98	M. Schumacher	D. Coulthard	J. Villeneuve
'99	M. Hakkinen	D. Coulthard	E. Irvine

STARTING GRID

M. SCHUMACHER FERRARI
1'17"514 (184,612)

(1) **D. COULTHARD** MCLAREN
1'17"886 (183,730)

M. HAKKINEN MCLAREN
1'17"922 (183,645)

(2) **R. SCHUMACHER** WILLIAMS
1'18"321 (182,710)

R. BARRICHELLO FERRARI
1'18"330 (182,689)

(3) **H.H. FRENTZEN** JORDAN
1'18"523 (182,240)

G. FISICHELLA BENETTON
1'18"607 (182,045)

(4) **J. BUTTON** WILLIAMS
1'18"699 (181,832)

M. SALO SAUBER
1'18"748 (181,719)

(5) **E. IRVINE** JAGUAR
1'19"008 (181,121)

A. WURZ BENETTON
1'19"259 (180,547)

(6) **J. TRULLI** JORDAN
1'19"266 (180,531)

P. DINIZ SAUBER
1'19"451 (180,111)

(7) **J. ALESI** PROST
1'19"626 (179,715)

P. DE LA ROSA ARROWS
1'19"897 (179,106)

(8) **J. VILLENEUVE** BAR
1'19"937 (179,016)

J. HERBERT JAGUAR
1'19"956 (178,973)

(9) **R. ZONTA** BAR
1'20"272 (178,269)

N. HEIDFELD PROST
1'20"481 (177,806)

(10) **J. VERSTAPPEN** ARROWS
1'20"609 (177,524)

M. GENE' MINARDI
1'20"654 (177,425)

(11) **G. MAZZACANE** MINARDI
1'20"905 (176,874)

Mission accomplished!

Qualifying saw a fifth pole position of the year for Michael Schumacher and a superb performance by the BMW-Williams duo of Ralf Schumacher in 4th and Jenson Button in 8th. Instead the BARs had a disastrous session with Villeneuve and Zonta 16th and 18th respectively.
Despite starting from row 2, Hakkinen rocketed away and at the first curve had already squeezed his way past Schumacher into the lead, a position he would hold until the chequered flag. Unfortunately this was one of the most boring GPs this year and the spectators waited anxiously for something to happen in the pit stops. But even the stops did not create much difficulty for the drivers, except for Ralf Schumacher who had a problem with a wheel.
Virtually nothing exciting happened in Hungary, with the exception of the retirement of the two Prosts (just for a change...!), a stop-go penalty for Minardi's Marc Gené and two spins by Herbert who then retired.
Mika Hakkinen completed his mission to overhaul Michael Schumacher's points lead and the German was now in a McLaren-Mercedes sandwich.
After 12 races and a triumphant start for Schumacher, the ball was firmly in the court of Hakkinen, who had a two-point lead over the Ferrari driver.

HIGHLIGHTS

• Minardi sporting director Cesare Fiorio left the Italian team a couple of days before the Hungarian GP.
In his 40-year career, Fiorio has also been sporting director for Ferrari, Ligier and Prost.

• Flavio Briatore confirmed Giancarlo Fisichella as Benetton's number 1 driver next year.
The Italian's team-mate will be Jenson Button, who has produced some outstanding performances in his debut year.

• Toyota top brass were out in full for the presentation of the F1 project, which will have its first shakedown tests in 2001 with Mika Salo.

RESULTS

	DRIVER	CAR	KPH	GAP
1	M. Hakkinen	McLaren	173,965	-
2	M. Schumacher	Ferrari	173,748	7"917
3	D. Coulthard	McLaren	173,733	8"455
4	R. Barrichello	Ferrari	172,760	44"157
5	R. Schumacher	Williams	172,590	50"437
6	H.H. Frentzen	Jordan	172,114	1'08"099
7	J. Trulli	Jordan	170,993	1 lap
8	E. Irvine	Jaguar	170,972	1 lap
9	J. Button	Williams	170,851	1 lap
10	M. Salo	Sauber	169,938	1 lap
11	A. Wurz	Benetton	169,749	1 lap
12	J. Villeneuve	BAR	169,371	2 laps
13	J. Verstappen	Arrows	168,380	2 laps
14	R. Zonta	BAR	167,250	2 laps
15	M. Gené	Minardi	166,392	3 laps
16	P. De La Rosa	Arrows	164,754	4 laps

RETIREMENTS

DRIVER	CAR	LAP
J. Alesi	Prost	11
N. Heidfeld	Prost	22
G. Fisichella	Benetton	31
P. Diniz	Sauber	62
J. Herbert	Jaguar	67
G. Mazzacane	Minardi	68

Schumacher 68

Barrichello 49

Hakkinen 74

Coulthard 61

Front-row starter Jarno Trulli (Jordan) followed by Jenson Button, who qualified one place behind on row 2. The two youngsters gave a good account of themselves but once again the podium was made up of the usual suspects: Michael, Mika and Ralf.

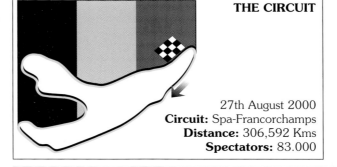

Belgian GP

	1°	2°	3°
'90	A. Senna	A. Prost	G. Berger
'91	A. Senna	G. Berger	N. Piquet
'92	M. Schumacher	N. Mansell	R. Patrese
'93	D. Hill	M. Schumacher	A. Prost
'94	D. Hill	M. Hakkinen	J. Verstappen
'95	M. Schumacher	D. Hill	M. Brundle
'96	M. Schumacher	J. Villeneuve	M. Hakkinen
'97	M. Schumacher	G. Fisichella	M. hakkinen
'98	D. Hill	R. Schumacher	J. Alesi
'99	D. Coulthard	M. Hakkinen	H.H. Frentzen

THE CIRCUIT

27th August 2000
Circuit: Spa-Francorchamps
Distance: 306,592 Kms
Spectators: 83.000

STARTING GRID

M. HAKKINEN McLAREN
1'50"646 (226,712) **(1)**

J. TRULLI JORDAN
1'51"419 (225,139)

J. BUTTON WILLIAMS
1'51"444 (225,089) **(2)**

M. SCHUMACHER FERRARI
1'51"552 (224,871)

D. COULTHARD McLAREN
1'51"587 (224,800) **(3)**

R. SCHUMACHER WILLIAMS
1'51"743 (224,487)

J. VILLENEUVE BAR
1'51"799 (224,374) **(4)**

H.H. FRENTZEN JORDAN
1'51"926 (224,120)

J. HERBERT JAGUAR
1'52"242 (223,489) **(5)**

R. BARRICHELLO FERRARI
1'52"444 (223,087)

G. FISICHELLA BENETTON
1'52"758 (222,466) **(6)**

E. IRVINE JAGUAR
1'52"885 (222,216)

R. ZONTA BAR
1'53"002 (221,985) **(7)**

N. HEIDFELD PROST
1'53"193 (221,611)

P. DINIZ SAUBER
1'53"211 (221,576) **(8)**

P. DE LA ROSA ARROWS
1'53"237 (221,525)

J. ALESI PROST
1'53"309 (221,384) **(9)**

M. SALO SAUBER
1'53"357 (221,290)

A. WURZ BENETTON
1'53"403 (221,200) **(10)**

J. VERSTAPPEN ARROWS
1'53"912 (220,212)

M. GENE' MINARDI
1'54"680 (218,737) **(11)**

G. MAZZACANE MINARDI
1'54"784 (218,539)

More McLaren!

Pole position, the 300 kph mark broken in the famous Eau Rouge Esses and a fantastic win for Mika Hakkinen, who increased his lead to 6 points over Schumacher. Schumacher's second place was entirely due to his talent and courage because the Maranello car was far inferior to the McLaren in performance terms. Jarno Trulli was a superb second quickest in qualifying on the ultra-fast Belgian circuit, ahead of an increasingly amazing Jenson Button. The race began in an unusual way, with all the cars lined up ready for a rolling start behind the safety car due to the wet conditions. Hakkinen had no problems in getting away, while behind Trulli and Button were already involved in a scrap. Schumacher then succeeded in passing them both between laps 4 and 5 but was unable to catch up on Hakkinen until lap 13 when the Finn had a high-speed spin and the Ferrari moved into the lead.
But the McLaren was much quicker than the Ferrari and lap after lap Hakkinen annulled Schumacher's lead.
The German was left helpless when the duo came up upon the BAR of Zonta in the middle of the track. Schumacher moved to the left to put Zonta between himself and Mika, but the Finn squeezed into the tiny space on the right and took them both in one go.
It was a spectacular move that left the Ferrari driver standing. Mika went on to win, Schumacher was second and his younger brother Ralf was third.

HIGHLIGHTS

- Minardi celebrated its 250th grand prix after making its debut in Brazil 1985 with Italian Pierluigi Martini. Three years later, Martini scored the first point for the Faenza-based team with 6th place in the US GP in Detroit. In 1990, the small Italian team was rewarded for years of effort with a front-row grid position at the US GP in Phoenix.

- 23 year-old German Nick Heidfeld, who currently drives for Prost, signed to race for the Swiss Sauber team in 2001.

RESULTS

	DRIVER	CAR	KPH	GAP
1	M. Hakkinen	McLaren	208,468	-
2	M. Schumacher	Ferrari	208,424	1"104
3	R. Schumacher	Williams	206,978	38"096
4	D. Coulthard	McLaren	206,777	43"281
5	J. Button	Williams	206,521	49"914
6	H.H. Frentzen	Jordan	206,286	55"984
7	J. Villeneuve	BAR	205,656	1'12"380
8	J. Herbert	Jaguar	205,067	1'27"808
9	M. Salo	Sauber	205,034	1'28"670
10	E. Irvine	Jaguar	204,924	1'31"555
11	P. Diniz	Sauber	204,826	1'34"123
12	R. Zonta	BAR	203,289	1 lap
13	A. Wurz	Benetton	202,404	1 lap
14	M. Gené	Minardi	201,459	1 lap
15	J. Verstappen	Arrows	200,078	1 lap
16	P. De La Rosa	Arrows	198,850	2 laps
17	G. Mazzacane	Minardi	196,127	2 laps

RETIREMENTS

DRIVER	CAR	LAP
J. Trulli	Jordan	4
G. Fisichella	Benetton	8
N. Heidfeld	Prost	12
J. Alesi	Prost	32
R. Barrichello	Ferrari	32

Australian GP | Brazilian GP | San Marino GP | British GP | Spanish GP | European GP | Monaco GP | Canadian GP | French GP | Austrian GP | German GP | Hungarian GP | Belgian GP | Italian GP | United States GP | Japanese GP | Malaysian GP

Schumacher 78
Barrichello 49
Hakkinen 80
Coulthard 61

A Ferrari 'heart' in front of the podium with Schumacher, Hakkinen and his brother Ralf. Irvine had a disappointing time at Monza and went out at the first chicane on lap 1. In the final photo, Jos Verstappen and Ricardo Zonta, who finished 4th and 6th respectively.

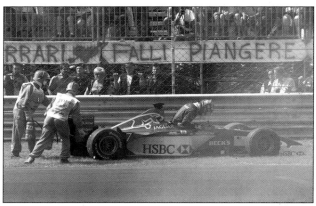

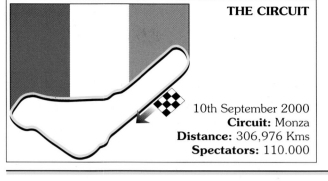

Italian GP

	1°	2°	3°
'90	A. Senna	A. Prost	G. Berger
'91	N. Mansell	A. Senna	A. Prost
'92	A. Senna	M. Brundle	M. Schumacher
'93	D. Hill	J. Alesi	M. Andretti
'94	D. Hill	G. Berger	M. Hakkinen
'95	J. Herbert	M. Hakkinen	H.H. Frentzen
'96	M. Schumacher	J. Alesi	M.Hakkinen
'97	D. Coulthard	J. Alesi	H.H. Frentzen
'98	M. Schumacher	E. Irvine	R. Schumacher
'99	H.H. Frentzen	R. Schumacher	M. Salo

THE CIRCUIT

10th September 2000
Circuit: Monza
Distance: 306,976 Kms
Spectators: 110.000

STARTING GRID

1.
M. SCHUMACHER FERRARI
1'23"770 (248,910)
R. BARRICHELLO FERRARI
1'23"797 (248,830)

2.
M. HAKKINEN McLAREN
1'23"967 (248,326)
J. VILLENEUVE BAR
1'24"238 (247,527)

3.
D. COULTHARD McLAREN
1'24"290 (247,375)
J. TRULLI JORDAN
1'24"477 (246,827)

4.
R. SCHUMACHER WILLIAMS
1'24"516 (246,713)
H.H. FRENTZEN JORDAN
1'24"786 (245,927)

5.
G. FISICHELLA BENETTON
1'24"789 (245,919)
P. DE LA ROSA ARROWS
1'24"814 (245,846)

6.
J. VERSTAPPEN ARROWS
1'24"820 (245,829)
J. BUTTON WILLIAMS
1'24"907 (245,577)

7.
A. WURZ BENETTON
1'25"150 (244,876)
E. IRVINE JAGUAR
1'25"251 (244,586)

8.
M. SALO SAUBER
1'25"322 (244,382)
P. DINIZ SAUBER
1'25"324 (244,377)

9.
R. ZONTA BAR
1'25"337 (244,340)
J. HERBERT JAGUAR
1'25"388 (244,194)

10.
J. ALESI PROST
1'25"558 (243,708)
N. HEIDFELD PROST
1'25"625 (243,518)

11.
M. GENE' MINARDI
1'26"336 (241,512)
G. MAZZACANE MINARDI
1'27"360 (238,681)

Schumacher King of Monza!

The championship was wide-open again and that was good for F1 in general. At Monza, Ferrari monopolised the front row with Hakkinen 3rd and Coulthard 5th. Villeneuve also had a great session, qualifying 4th.

A tragedy was just avoided in the race, not as was feared at the first chicane, which was modified this year, but at the Variante Roggia before the Curva di Lesmo. Frentzen arrived like a rocket and hit his Jordan team-mate Trulli, involving Barrichello and Coulthard in the incident as well. Wheels and wings went flying everywhere, while a cloud of gravel prevented the drivers behind from seeing anything. De la Rosa collided with Herbert, arrived on the scene in the middle of the dust with his Arrows, and looped over to almost end up on top of the Brazilian's Ferrari. None of the drivers were hurt in the pile-up but it was a tragedy all the same because a Monza fire marshal, one of 230 volunteers around the track, was killed when a flying wheel from one of the cars hit him full on behind the barrier.

The safety car came out and kept the 15 remaining cars behind in single file for 10 laps while the debris was cleared up. After that, Schumacher dominated and only lost the lead to Hakkinen during his stop. It was a triumphant victory and it sparked off the usual track invasion by tifosi. Thousands of red flags celebrated the 'King of Monza', who stepped up onto the podium with Hakkinen and his brother Ralf. Jos Verstappen was a superb fourth after a determined but prudent race.

HIGHLIGHTS

• Honda celebrated its 200th grand prix at Monza, the circuit where it won in 1967 with John Surtees, who passed reigning world champion Jack Brabham at the final curve on the last lap.

• With his win, Schumacher took his personal total at the legendary Autodromo di Monza to three, the same as Fangio ('53, '54 and '55), Moss ('56, '57 and '59), Peterson ('73, '74 and '76) and Piquet ('83, '86 and '87).

• Finally a good result for Alexander Wurz, who scored his first points this year with 5th place at Monza.

RESULTS

	DRIVER	CAR	KPH	GAP
1	M. Schumacher	Ferrari	210,286	-
2	M. Hakkinen	McLaren	210,134	3"810
3	R. Schumacher	Williams	208,208	52"432
4	J. Verstappen	Arrows	207,913	99"938
5	A. Wurz	Benetton	207,621	1'07"426
6	R. Zonta	BAR	207,548	1'09"293
7	M. Salo	Sauber	206,125	1 lap
8	P. Diniz	Sauber	206,895	1 lap
9	M. Gené	Minardi	205,643	1 lap
10	G. Mazzacane	Minardi	205,988	1 lap
11	G. Fisichella	Benetton	204,976	1 lap
12	J. Alesi	Prost	201,535	2 laps

RETIREMENTS

DRIVER	CAR	LAP
D. Coulthard	McLaren	0
P. De La Rosa	Arrows	0
H.H. Frentzen	Jordan	0
J. Trulli	Jordan	0
R. Barrichello	Ferrari	0
E. Irvine	Jaguar	0
J. Herbert	Jaguar	1
J. Button	Williams	10
J. Villeneuve	BAR	14
N. Heidfeld	Prost	15

Schumacher 88

Barrichello 55

Hakkinen 80

Coulthard 63

Schumacher's uncontrollable joy at the end of the race as he is embraced by Barrichello. In the other photos: Schumacher's risky move to overtake Coulthard and the moment of truth for Hakkinen as his engine bursts into flames.

United States GP

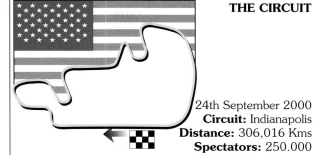

THE CIRCUIT

24th September 2000
Circuit: Indianapolis
Distance: 306,016 Kms
Spectators: 250.000

STARTING GRID

M. SCHUMACHER FERRARI 1'14"266 (203,205)	**(1)**	**D. COULTHARD** MCLAREN 1'14"392 (202,861)
M. HAKKINEN MCLAREN 1'14"428 (202,762)	**(2)**	**R. BARRICHELLO** FERRARI 1'14"600 (202,295)
J. TRULLI JORDAN 1'15"006 (201,200)	**(3)**	**J. BUTTON** WILLIAMS 1'15"017 (201,170)
H.H. FRENTZEN JORDAN 1'15"067 (201,036)	**(4)**	**J. VILLENEUVE** BAR 1'15"317 (200,369)
P. DINIZ SAUBER 1'15"418 (200,101)	**(5)**	**R. SCHUMACHER** WILLIAMS 1'15"484 (199,926)
A. WURZ BENETTON 1'15"762 (199,192)	**(6)**	**R. ZONTA** BAR 1'15"784 (199,134)
J. VERSTAPPEN ARROWS 1'15"808 (199,071)	**(7)**	**M. SALO** SAUBER 1'15"881 (198,880)
G. FISICHELLA BENETTON 1'15"907 (198,812)	**(8)**	**N. HEIDFELD** PROST 1'16"060 (198,412)
E. IRVINE JAGUAR 1'16"098 (198,313)	**(9)**	**P. DE LA ROSA** ARROWS 1'16"143 (198,196)
J. HERBERT JAGUAR 1'16"225 (197,982)	**(10)**	**J. ALESI** PROST 1'16"471 (197,345)
G. MAZZACANE MINARDI 1'16"809 (196,477)	**(11)**	**M. GENE'** MINARDI 1'17"161 (195,581)

Ferrari Stars and Stripes !

May 1952: Ferrari arrives in the USA with Alberto Ascari to take part in the Indianapolis 500 Miles race, but the expedition was a disaster and the car, a Ferrari 375, totally unsuitable. September 2000: Ferrari arrives at the legendary 'Brickyard' for the second time. This time everything was prepared in detail and it was evident right from the start of free practice. Things went even better in qualifying with Schumacher on pole and Barrichello 3rd, but the real masterstroke came in the race. Schumacher started well, but Coulthard elbowed his way into the first curve ahead of him. The German had no idea that Coulthard had jumped the start and was about to be penalised with a stop-go penalty. Schumacher then managed to muscle his way ahead of Coulthard a few laps later and he pulled out a massive lead on Mika Hakkinen, with a little help from an early pit-stop by the Finn who came back out on slick tyres.
Mika then began to close the gap at a rate of more than one second a lap, but this all went up in smoke... together with his McLaren engine on lap 26.
It was looking easy for Schumacher, but the German lost concentration five laps from the end and spun his Ferrari, but recovered. Barrichello was runner-up, followed by Frentzen in the Jordan, who must have breathed a huge sigh of relief after the Monza race. Former Indy 500 winner Villeneuve had a great race, exciting the 250,000 spectators with late braking moves and spins as he tried to grab third from Frentzen in the final laps. But the day belonged to Schumacher and Ferrari, who were back in the lead of the Drivers' and Manufacturers' standings.

HIGHLIGHTS

• Alain Prost confirmed he had secured an engine deal with Ferrari for 2001, the same as Sauber. After a difficult season, the former Ferrari driver can now be optimistic about next year.

• Disastrous pit-stop for Minardi, when Mazzacane knocked over one of his mechanics.

• Another superb performance by Jenson Button, who qualified sixth, while the weekend was a disappointment for Giancarlo Fisichella, who qualified fifteenth and was promptly slammed by Flavio Briatore for his scarce commitment.

RESULTS

	DRIVER	CAR	KPH	GAP
1	M. Schumacher	Ferrari	190,240	-
2	R. Barrichello	Ferrari	189,843	12"118
3	H.H. Frentzen	Jordan	189,671	17"368
4	J. Villeneuve	BAR	189,653	17"936
5	D. Coulthard	McLaren	189,298	28"813
6	R. Zonta	BAR	188,557	51"694
7	E. Irvine	Jaguar	187,932	1'11"115
8	P. Diniz	Sauber	187,614	1 lap
9	N. Heidfeld	Prost	187,426	1 lap
10	A. Wurz	Benetton	187,380	1 lap
11	J. Herbert	Jaguar	187,341	1 lap
12	M. Gené	Minardi	186,546	1 lap

RETIREMENTS

DRIVER	CAR	LAP
J. Trulli	Jordan	12
J. Button	Williams	14
M. Salo	Sauber	18
M. Hakkinen	McLaren	25
J. Verstappen	Arrows	34
G. Fisichella	Benetton	44
P. De La Rosa	Arrows	45
R. Schumacher	Williams	58
G. Mazzacane	Minardi	59
J. Alesi	Prost	64

Australian GP · Brazilian GP · San Marino GP · British GP · Spanish GP · European GP · Monaco GP · Canadian GP · French GP · Austrian GP · German GP · Hungarian GP · Belgian GP · Italian GP · United States GP · Japanese GP · Malaysian GP

Schumacher 98
Barrichello 58
Hakkinen 86
Coulthard 67

Hakkinen powered into the lead of the Japanese GP after Schumacher swerved off the line. 53 laps later, the German was embraced by Barrichello amidst scenes of joy on the podium and in the pits.

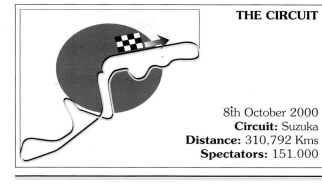

Japanese GP

	1°	2°	3°
'90	N. Piquet	R. Moreno	A. Suzuki
'91	G. Berger	A. Senna	R. Patrese
'92	R. Patrese	G. Berger	M. Brundle
'93	A. Senna	A. Prost	M. Hakkinen
'94	D. Hill	M. Schumacher	J. Alesi
'95	M. Schumacher	M. Hakkinen	J.Herbert
'96	D. Hill	M. Schumacher	M. Hakkinen
'97	M. Schumacher	H.H. Frentzen	E. Irvine
'98	M. Hakkinen	E. Irvine	D. Coulthard
'99	M. Hakkinen	M. Schumacher	E. Irvine

THE CIRCUIT

8th October 2000
Circuit: Suzuka
Distance: 310,792 Kms
Spectators: 151.000

STARTING GRID

M. SCHUMACHER FERRARI 1'35"825 (220,302)	**M. HAKKINEN** MCLAREN 1'35"834 (220,281)
D. COULTHARD MCLAREN 1'36"236 (219,361)	**R. BARRICHELLO** FERRARI 1'36"330 (219,147)
J. BUTTON WILLIAMS 1'36"628 (218,471)	**R. SCHUMACHER** WILLIAMS 1'36"788 (218,110)
E. IRVINE JAGUAR 1'36"899 (217,860)	**H.H. FRENTZEN** JORDAN 1'37"243 (217,089)
J. VILLENEUVE BAR 1'37"267 (217,036)	**J. HERBERT** JAGUAR 1'37"329 (216,897)
A. WURZ BENETTON 1'37"348 (216,855)	**G. FISICHELLA** BENETTON 1'37"479 (216,564)
P. DE LA ROSA ARROWS 1'37"652 (216,180)	**J. VERSTAPPEN** ARROWS 1'37"674 (216,131)
J. TRULLI JORDAN 1'37"679 (216,120)	**N. HEIDFELD** PROST 1'38"141 (215,103)
J. ALESI PROST 1'38"209 (214,954)	**R. ZONTA** BAR 1'38"269 (214,823)
M. SALO SAUBER 1'38"490 (214,341)	**P. DINIZ** SAUBER 1'38"576 (214,154)
M. GENE' MINARDI 1'39"972 (211,163)	**G. MAZZACANE** MINARDI 1'40"462 (210,133)

RESULTS

	DRIVER	CAR	KPH	GAP
1	M. Schumacher	Ferrari	207,447	-
2	M. Hakkinen	McLaren	207,376	1"837
3	D. Coulthard	McLaren	204,792	1'09"914
4	R. Barrichello	Ferrari	204,445	1'19"191
5	J. Button	Williams	204,202	1'25"694
6	J. Villeneuve	BAR	203,223	1 lap
7	J. Herbert	Jaguar	203,189	1 lap
8	E. Irvine	Jaguar	203,130	1 lap
9	R. Zonta	BAR	201,561	1 lap
10	M. Salo	Sauber	200,726	1 lap
11	P. Diniz	Sauber	200,477	1 lap
12	P. De La Rosa	Arrows	200,434	1 lap
13	J. Trulli	Jordan	200,307	1 lap
14	G. Fisichella	Benetton	200,288	1 lap
15	G. Mazzacane	Minardi	196,049	2 laps

RETIREMENTS

DRIVER	CAR	LAP
J. Verstappen	Arrows	9
J. Alesi	Prost	19
H.H. Frentzen	Jordan	29
A. Wurz	Benetton	37
N. Heidfeld	Prost	41
R. Schumacher	Williams	41
M. Gené	Minardi	46

A dream comes true !

Ferrari finally clinched the Drivers' title after 21 years of hopes, dreams and expectations! For millions of tifosi and citizens of Maranello, the title arrived at dawn and came from a race that in recent years had produced numerous disappointments for Ferrari. This time they made no mistake and Schumacher clinched the championship with a record number of wins for the Prancing Horse team. The start appeared to confirm Ferrari's negative tradition at Suzuka. Michael swerved away and pulled over towards Hakkinen who just managed to squeeze through before the first curve. The Finn led for lap after lap but Schumacher was always within striking distance. It was a tactical race until the second and final pit stop when Michael came out four seconds in front, a lead he succeeded in maintaining until the chequered flag. The Japanese Grand Prix was all about Schumacher and Hakkinen and the others were only in the race when they had to move over to let the championship contenders through. It wasn't a Grand Prix; it was a war of nerves in a tense climate. An error or a breakdown could have decided the title, but neither driver put a foot wrong, a sign of two great champions, and in the end a deserved victory went to Schumacher. It was a victory for the boys in red, who for years had packed their bags at the final race of the year and headed home with disappointment in their hearts. It was a victory for the company that has helped to make Formula One great over the years. And finally it was a victory for the Prancing Horse and its founder, Enzo Ferrari. For the record, Coulthard was third, Barrichello fourth, Button fifth and Villeneuve sixth.

	1°	2°	3°
'99	E. Irvine	M. Schumacher	M. Hakkinen

THE CIRCUIT
22nd October 2000
Circuit: Sepang
Distance: 310,408 Kms
Spectators: 99.000

STARTING GRID

1
M. SCHUMACHER FERRARI
1'37"397 (204,881)
M. HAKKINEN McLAREN
1'37"860 (203,912)

2
D. COULTHARD McLAREN
1'37"889 (203,851)
R. BARRICHELLO FERRARI
1'37"896 (203,837)

3
A. WURZ BENETTON
1'38"644 (202,291)
J. VILLENEUVE BAR
1'38"653 (202,273)

4
E. IRVINE JAGUAR
1'38"696 (202,184)
R. SCHUMACHER WILLIAMS
1'38"739 (202,096)

5
J. TRULLI JORDAN
1'38"909 (201,749)
H.H. FRENTZEN JORDAN
1'38"988 (201,588)

6
R. ZONTA BAR
1'39"158 (201,242)
J. HERBERT JAGUAR
1'39"331 (200,892)

7
G. FISICHELLA BENETTON
1'39"387 (200,779)
P. DE LA ROSA ARROWS
1'39"443 (200,666)

8
J. VERSTAPPEN ARROWS
1'39"489 (200,573)
J. BUTTON WILLIAMS
1'39"563 (200,424)

9
M. SALO SAUBER
1'39"591 (200,368)
J. ALESI PROST
1'40"065 (199,418)

10
N. HEIDFELD PROST
1'40"148 (199,253)
P. DINIZ SAUBER
1'40"521 (198,514)

11
M. GENE' MINARDI
1'40"662 (198,236)
G. MAZZACANE MINARDI
1'42"078 (195,486)

Malaysian GP

PETRONAS MALAYSIAN GRAND PRIX KUALA LUMPUR 2000

Champion Schumacher takes Ferrari to Constructors' title!

The final round of the year in Malaysia turned into triumph for Ferrari. After claiming his ninth pole position of the season, Schumacher then went on to win the Sepang race, giving Ferrari its second consecutive Constructors' title.
For the record, Ferrari equalled its highest number of pole positions (9 for Schumacher, 1 for Barrichello) held by Lauda-Regazzoni in the 1974 championship. With 9 wins, Schumacher also beat the 1952/1953 record held by Ascari and team-mates who won 7 races. At the start of the Malaysian GP, Hakkinen made things easy for Ferrari by rolling away from the line and picking up a 10-second stop-go penalty.

Mika sportingly moved aside to let Coulthard through into the lead and the Scot immediately pulled out a 5-second advantage over Schumacher.
But the German's Ferrari was carrying more fuel than the McLaren and he could delay his refuelling stop.
Coulthard refuelled but Schumacher stayed out for six more laps before his stop.
When he returned to the track he had a few seconds' lead over the number 2 McLaren, which was closing lap after lap.
But the German was controlling the race and he took the chequered flag almost one second ahead of Coulthard.
Barrichello, Hakkinen, Villeneuve and Irvine took the remaining top 6 positions.
Irvine's team-mate Johnny Herbert, who was taking part in his last F1 race, had a major crash when the rear suspension of his Jaguar broke. The impact was a big one but luckily Herbert emerged with just bruising.
With Sepang a sea of red banners and flags for the Scuderia's victory, the entire Ferrari team started the celebrations off by appearing in red wigs. In a sporting gesture, the McLaren team also joined in the fun by wearing red wigs when they handed over the numbers 1 and 2 to Jean Todt.

RESULTS

	DRIVER	CAR	KPH	GAP
1	M. Schumacher	Ferrari	194,199	-
2	D. Coulthard	McLaren	194,175	"732
3	R. Barrichello	Ferrari	193,579	18"444
4	M. Hakkinen	McLaren	193,016	35"269
5	J. Villeneuve	BAR	191,843	1'10"692
6	E. Irvine	Jaguar	191,781	1'12"568
7	A. Wurz	Benetton	191,231	1'29"314
8	M. Salo	Sauber	190,517	1 lap
9	G. Fisichella	Benetton	190,383	1 lap
10	J. Verstappen	Arrows	190,165	1 lap
11	J. Alesi	Prost	188,658	1 lap
12	J. Trulli	Jordan	188.050	1 lap
13	G. Mazzacane	Minardi	185,556	6 laps

RETIREMENTS

DRIVER	CAR	LAP
N. Heidfeld	Prost	0
P. De La Rosa	Arrows	0
P. Diniz	Sauber	0
H.H. Frentzen	Jordan	7
J. Button	Williams	18
M. Gené	Minardi	36
R. Schumacher	Williams	43
R. Zonta	BAR	46
J. Herbert	Jaguar	48

M. Schumacher (D) - Ferrari
Ferrari

2000 World Championship: Drivers & Constructors

Drivers	Australian GP	Brazilian GP	San Marino GP	British GP	Spanish GP	European GP	Monaco GP	Canadian GP	French GP	Austrian GP	German GP	Hungarian GP	Belgian GP	Italian GP	United States GP	Japanese GP	Malaysian GP	TOTAL POINTS
M. Schumacher	10	10	10	4	2	10	-	10	-	-	-	6	6	10	10	10	10	108
M. Hakkinen	-	-	6	6	10	6	1	3	6	10	6	10	10	6	-	6	3	89
D. Coulthard	-	-	4	10	6	4	10	-	10	6	4	4	3	-	2	4	6	73
R. Barrichello	6	-	3	-	4	3	6	6	4	4	10	3	-	-	6	3	4	62
R. Schumacher	4	2	-	3	3	-	-	-	2	-	-	2	4	4	-	-	-	24
G. Fisichella	2	6	-	-	2	4	4	-	-	-	-	-	-	-	-	-	-	18
J. Villeneuve	3	-	2	-	-	-	-	-	3	3	-	-	-	-	3	1	2	17
J. Button	-	1	-	2	-	-	-	-	-	2	3	-	2	-	-	2	-	12
H.H. Frentzen	-	4	-	-	1	-	-	-	-	-	-	1	1	-	4	-	-	11
M. Salo	-	-	1	-	-	-	2	-	-	1	2	-	-	-	-	-	-	6
J. Trulli	-	3	-	1	-	-	-	-	1	1	-	-	-	-	-	-	-	6
J. Verstappen	-	-	-	-	-	-	2	-	-	-	-	-	-	3	-	-	-	5
E. Irvine	-	-	-	-	-	-	3	-	-	-	-	-	-	-	-	-	1	4
R. Zonta	1	-	-	-	-	-	-	-	-	-	-	-	-	-	1	1	-	3
P. De La Rosa	-	-	-	-	-	1	-	-	-	-	1	-	-	-	-	-	-	2
A. Wurz	-	-	-	-	-	-	-	-	-	-	-	-	-	-	2	-	-	2

Constructors

Ferrari	16	10	13	4	6	13	6	16	4	4	10	9	6	10	16	13	14	170
McLaren	-	-	10	16	16	10	11	3	16	6	10	14	13	6	2	10	9	152
Williams	4	3	-	5	3	-	-	-	2	2	3	2	6	4	-	2	-	36
Benetton	2	6	-	-	-	2	4	4	-	-	-	-	-	2	-	-	-	20
Bar	4	-	2	-	-	-	-	-	3	3	-	-	-	1	4	1	2	20
Jordan	-	7	-	1	1	-	1	-	1	-	1	1	-	4	-	-	-	17
Arrows	-	-	-	-	-	1	-	2	-	-	1	-	-	3	-	-	-	7
Sauber	-	-	1	-	-	-	2	-	-	1	2	-	-	-	-	-	-	6
Jaguar	-	-	-	-	-	-	3	-	-	-	-	-	-	-	-	-	1	4

World Champions 1950-2000

N. Farina	(I - Alfa Romeo)	1950	
J.M. Fangio	(RA - Alfa Romeo)	1951	
A. Ascari	(I - Ferrari)	1952	
A. Ascari	(I - Ferrari)	1953	
J.M. Fangio	(RA - Maserati, Mercedes)	1954	
J.M. Fangio	(RA - Mercedes)	1955	
J.M. Fangio	(RA - Ferrari)	1956	
J.M. Fangio	(RA - Maserati)	1957	
M. Hawthorn	(GB - Ferrari)	1958	Vanwal
J. Brabham	(AUS - Cooper)	1959	Cooper
J. BrabhaM	(AUS - Cooper)	1960	Cooper
P. Hill	(USA - Ferrari)	1961	Ferrari
G. Hill	(GB - Brm)	1962	Brm
J. Clark	(GB - Lotus)	1963	Lotus
J. Surtees	(GB - Ferrari)	1964	Ferrari
J. Clark	(GB - Lotus)	1965	Lotus
J. Brabham	(AUS - Brabham)	1966	Brabham
D. Hulme	(NZ - Brabham)	1967	Brabham
G. Hill	(GB - Lotus)	1968	Lotus
J. Stewart	(GB - Matra)	1969	Matra
J. Rindt	(A - Lotus)	1970	Lotus
J. Stewart	(GB - Tyrrell)	1971	Tyrrell
E. Fittipaldi	(BR - Lotus)	1972	Lotus
J. Stewart	(GB - Tyrrell)	1973	Lotus
E. Fittipaldi	(BR - McLaren)	1974	McLaren
N. Lauda	(A - Ferrari)	1975	Ferrari
J. Hunt	(GB - McLaren)	1976	Ferrari
N. Lauda	(A - Ferrari)	1977	Ferrari
M. Andretti	(USA - Lotus)	1978	Lotus
J. Scheckter	(ZA - Ferrari)	1979	Ferrari
A. Jones	(AUS - Williams)	1980	Williams
N. Piquet	(BR - Brabham)	1981	Williams
K. Rosberg	(SF - Williams)	1982	Ferrari
N. Piquet	(BR - Brabham)	1983	Ferrari
N. Lauda	(A - McLaren)	1984	McLaren
A. Prost	(F - McLaren)	1985	McLaren
A. Prost	(F - McLaren)	1986	Williams
N. Piquet	(BR - Williams)	1987	Williams
A. Senna	(BR - McLaren)	1988	McLaren
A. Prost	(F - McLaren)	1989	McLaren
A. Senna	(BR - McLaren)	1990	McLaren
A. Senna	(BR - McLaren)	1991	McLaren
N. Mansell	(GB - Williams)	1992	Williams
A. Prost	(F - Williams)	1993	Williams
M. Schumacher	(D - Benetton)	1994	Williams
M. Schumacher	(D - Benetton)	1995	Benetton
D. Hill	(GB - Williams)	1996	Williams
J. Villeneuve	(CDN - Williams)	1997	Williams
M. Hakkinen	(FIN - McLaren)	1998	McLaren
M. Hakkinen	(FIN - McLaren)	1999	Ferrari
M. Schumacher	(D - Ferrari)	2000	Ferrari

2000 World Championship in brief

	POLE POSITION	WINS	RETIREMENTS	FAST LAPS IN RACE
M. Schumacher	9	9	4	2
M. Hakkinen	5	4	3	9
D. Coulthard	2	3	2	3
R. Barrichello	1	1	4	3